NEW STRATEGIES FOR SUSTAINABLE ARCHITECTURE

ECOLOGICAL BUILDINGS

The Deutsche Nationalbibliothek lists this publication in
the Deutsche Nationalbibliografie; detailed bibliographic
data are available on the Internet at http://dnb.dnb.de

ISBN 978-3-03768-268-5
© 2021 by Braun Publishing AG
www.braun-publishing.ch

1st edition 2021

Editor: Editorial Office van Uffelen
Editorial staff and layout: Marina Kuhn, Sarah Stelzer
Graphic concept: Michaela Prinz, Berlin
Reproduction: Bild1Druck GmbH, Berlin

Cover front: Hiroyuki Oki (image), URBAN PLATFORM
architects (plan)
Cover back (from left to right, from above to below):
Lin Ho Photography, P. Caumes, Kaori Ichikawa

DORIAN LUCAS

NEW STRATEGIES FOR SUSTAINABLE ARCHITECTURE

ECOLOGICAL BUILDINGS

BRAUN

CONTENTS

PREFACE
NUMEROUS STANDARDS, MULTIPLE APPROACHES AND CREATIVE SOLUTIONS

Sustainable architecture – with its direct predecessors – is a topic for more than 50 years now, and it is still far from being fully discussed. Rather, a Babylonian diversity has developed in the meantime, a diversity of stylistic languages as well as a diversity of requirements, standards and certificates, of dos and don'ts that would cover a book of several hundred pages. What began with an interest in alternative ways of living, in responsability and with a certain degree of anarchy now encompasses sophisticated high-tech, Building Information Modeling and the question of human rights in supply chains. Measured against this, everything that is created should at least be "passive" by now. Especially when you consider that the vast majority of buildings that will exist in 2121 have already been built.

In the late 1960s, this development towards sustainable architecture as a whole remained imperceptible. Although there had already been warnings of environmental crises in the 1950s, these only found a broader resonance with the hippie movement spreading from the USA in the second half of the 1960s. In the search for alternative lifestyles, people rediscovered dwellings that had previously been considered backward. At the same time, criticism of the late modern city through, for example, "The death and life of great American Cities" by Jane Jacobs (1961) and "Inhospitality of our Cities" by Alexander Mitscherlich (1965) led to a critique of its construction methods. A pre-modern construction method was often found in the countryside or, among others, in the work of low-tech architects such as Hassan Fathis (New Barris Village in Egypt, starting in 1967), who sought a culture-specific construction method in this. But also an increasing awareness of health issues led to a rethinking in the long run: The physician Hubert Palm founded with numerous lectures in the 1960s what today is known as Building Biology, probably the oldest approach to Sustainable Architecture.

His thoughts were published in 1975 in "The Healthy House", right between the oil crises of 1974 and 1978 and when the Club of Rome had already pointed out "The Limits to Growth" for the first time (1972). Baum was essentially about the health effects of building materials and interrelationships and interactions between the building, the user (occupant) and its environment. The rise of the modern nature conservation movement, which for example in the American conservation movement already had precursors in the 19th century, became more international in the 1970s: In 1971, for example, the Friends of the Earth came into being as an international federation of national associations. At the same time, the city was renaturalized in a consumer-critical way on a small scale: In 1972, for example, the Street Farmhouse was created in Eltham, London, by the group Street Farm.

The tendency toward internationalization and institutionalization defined the following two decades. In the 1980s, it was above all the low-tech movement that drew attention to itself with earthwork or pisé buildings (Malcom Wells, Arthur Quambie, Jourda et Perraudin). With the use of passive solar energy, however, an analytical and technical standpoint was already taken in architecture (Thomas Herzog). Increasingly, social issues (social design, participation) played a role when, for example, the Bauhäusle in Stuttgart-Vaihingen, a student dormitory in Germany, was built by more than 200 students under the supervision of the architects Peter Sulzer and Peter Hübner by 1983. This was also in line with

experienced an enormous boom in the 1980s, Rolf Disch's Heliotrop in Freibug-Vauban became the first energy-plus house in 1994 as a solar revolving tree house, while hardly any zero-energy houses existed. Between 1999 and 2001, the CEPHEUS (Cost Efficient Passive Houses as European Standards) program was responsible for the construction of 221 residential units in five European countries. This increased the total number of passive houses threefold. But passive did not necessarily have to be ecological or sustainable; in fact, it referred only to the energy balance in the period of use. At that time, the energy that went into the building during construction was hardly cosidered, nor

the self-image of the Green parties that emerged from the various movements, including conservative environmental conservationist. In the 1990s they gained power in modern democracies of the Western world. It was in 1988 that Wolfgang Feist, together with Swedish professor Bo Adamson, who first defined what a passive house should entail. In 1991 Feist designed the first Passivhaus in Darmstadt-Kranichstein according to this.

At the beginning of the new decade, the Building Research Establishment in the United Kingdom published BREEAM (Building Research Establishment Environmental Assessment Methodology) in 1990 as the world's leading, internationally applied assessment system for ecological and building performance. After solar technology had

was the water consumed, the soil sealed, and the term carbon footprint, which has been known since 1994. In 1996, the European Charter for Solar Energy in Architecture and Urban Planning was drawn up. Jourda et Perraudin built the Mont-Cenis Academy in Herne in 1999 as an extremely flexible and practical city under a glass skin, which supports 10,000 square meters of solar collectors. The Eden Project in Cornwall, England, was realized in the second half of the 1990s by Grimshaw. The same architect built the water-cooled British Pavilion at Expo 92 in Seville, the hottest city in Europe. Increasingly, high-tech architecture began to focus on ecological aspects – in addition to Grimshaw, for example, Norman Foster with the Reichstag dome in Berlin (1999) or Kenneth Yeang with the green skyscraper Menara Mesiniaga in Kuala Lumpur (1992).

In 1993, pioneers of ecology such as Norman Foster, Renzo Piano, Richard Rogers and Thomas Herzog joined to form the READ Group (Renewable Energy in Architecture and Design). The double-skin façade – with precursors in the early 20th century – designed to serve as a ventilated climate buffer, became the building of choice for a time. In 1997, the Kyoto Protocol succeeded the Rio de Janeiro Earth Summit in 1992, and since 2015 it has been replaced by the Paris Agreement. At the end of the millennium, LEED (Leadership in Energy and Environmental Design) from the U.S. Green Building Council joined BREEAM in 1998, and WorldGBC was subsequently founded in 1999. In the meantime, numerous associ-

as early as 1884 by Lucien Lévy-Bruhl in the book "L'idee de responsabilité" and became a key concept in ethics after World War II – entered the architectural debate after the turn of the millennium and led to the phase of sustainable building after the building biology phase (1970/80s) and the ecological phase (1980/90s). The idea of sustainability originated as early as the 18th century, when it was thought that mankind was threatening to cut itself off from the most important raw material – firewood from the forest – through excessive use since the 16th century. From this debate, forestry science established itself in the second half of the 18th century. The new aspects of sustainability were also re-

ations and countries had adopted their own catalogs of requirements and measures, applying a wide variety of criteria. Some of the differences are, for example, due to climate while others are almost impossible to understand. Regarding town planning, Michael Sorkin followed Rem Koolhaas' "Delirious New York" (1978) with a geomorphic, ecological city growth as a role model for the upcoming century.

The dawn of the new millennium brought official recognition to sustainable architecture with the bestowal of the Pritzker Prize to Glen Murcutt in 2002, known for his Australian villas using natural building materials. Wang Shu, Pritzker Prize winner of 2012 with the Ningbo Museum (2008), is known for using materials from demolished buildings; Alejandro Aravena, winner of 2016, brought in the aspect of a social conscience and participation; for Balkrishna Doshi, winner of 2018, responsibility plays a major role alongside ecology. The ethical and moral aspect of responsibility – which was discussed

flected in the new DGNB certificate of the German Sustainable Building Council, founded in 2007. This certificate not only included socio-cultural factors, but also ergonomic and economic aspects, the complete life cycle of a building from the project development phase to dismantling, land use, site quality and the carbon footprint. In addition, this certificate has been designed from the outset to be adaptable to different regional requirements. In the long run, this concept would offer the possibility to unify LEED, REEAM, HQE (France), CASBEE (Japan), Green Star (Australia) or all the other certificates into one system. However, while environmental requirements simply have to be fulfilled, these certificates are voluntary on the one hand, and on the other hand they are associated with immense time and cost expenditures. Therefore, the decision to apply for them is always an economic one, weighing up the costs and benefits. In 2012, the Cradle To Cradle association was founded, an idea that German chemist Michael Braungart and US architect

William McDonough had been pursuing since the 1990s and published in 2002. Since then, the term – and the certificate of the same name, awarded by the non-profit Cradle To Cradle Products Innovation Institute starting in 2010 – has become an important part of the sustainable debate. Although the complete and single-variety reuse of all materials is of course not new. In Singapore, the Green Mark Scheme has been successful since 2005: This sustainability certification decides on subsidies or tax benefits for new buildings. In one of the most densely populated cities in the world, every square meter of green space destroyed on the building site by new construction must be replaced, so that green spaces

that was already envisioned in the Brandt Report 1980, in context of the North-South conflict. No wonder, then, that a generation after the next called for acceleration in sustainable development: On August 20, 2018, Greta Thunberg, then a 15-year-old climate protection activist, refused to attend class and thus initiated the Fridays for Future-movement, which took on completely unexpected proportions in no time at all. Their demands definitely also affect the building industry, every developer and every architect. What consequences the demand for sustainable architecture has for the concrete building project can only be decided in each individual case, so a material with a large amount of embodied

are now being increased through architecture. The greening of buildings took off in particular in the wake of Patric Blanc's first murs végétaux at designer Andrée Putman's Pershing Hall hotel in Paris in 2001. While climbing plants had of course existed on façades before, Blanc opened up a targeted design by using ground-cover plants in vertical gardens. While these are more selective interventions, large-scale developments were also undertaken after 2000: Freiburg-Vauban in Germany (already from 1998), the SolarCity in Linz, Austria (since 2004), or the emission-free city of Masdar in the Emirate of Abu Dhabi (since 2008) are well-known examples. Masdar is home to the International Renewable Energy Agency, founded in 2009, an organization

energy (structural steel 57,000 kWh/m²) may be more sustainable in individual cases than one with a smaller amount (sand lime brick, for 350 kWh/m², timber 180 kWh/m²) if correspondingly less mass is needed, the building as a high-rise then seals less soil or lasts longer. And the aesthetic value is also an ecological value, because a building that is pleasing or even just different from the average has a greater probability of lasting longer and is therefore already superior to many others in its carbon footprint. And so, with very different approaches, this book may help to rethink your planning, find new approaches, or think about where you can do something better yourself.

Jean Nouvel and Patric Blanc, 2008, Musée du quai Branly, Paris, France (picture credit: Chris van Uffelen)
Foster+Partners, 1999, Dome of the Bundestag im Reichstag, Berlin, Germany (picture credit: Chris van Uffelen)
Grimshaw & Partners, 2001, The Eden Project Biomes (2001) and The Core (2005), Cornwall, United Kingdom (picture credit: cowbridge.co.uk / wikimedia commons, CC-BY-3.0)
Safdi Architects, 2018, Jewel Changi Airport, Singapore (picture credit: Chris van Uffelen)

FACTORY IN THE FOREST
DESIGN UNIT ARCHITECTS

Location: Lorong Perindustrian Bukit Minyak 21, 14100 Simpang Ampat, Penang, Malaysia |
Completion: 2017 | **Client:** Paramit Malaysia | **Eco engineering:** IEN Consultants | **Building type:** corporate | **GFA:** 15,000 m² | **Photos:** Lin Ho Photography

Factory in the Forest is an office for an US electronics company specializing in medical equipment. The five-acre site is conceived as a forest that penetrates, surrounds and steps over the building creating maximum contact with nature – green, breeze, scent, sound, touch. The plant consists of four main elements: car park, office, courtyard and production. An over-sailing canopy, supported by a forest of slender columns creates unity to the office, courtyard and car park while giving protection to these spaces and functions from the tropical sun. From project onset, the client wanted an energy efficient and climatically responsive building, therefore environmental and sustainability were integral to the design process. The cardinal sustainable design principles were energy efficiency, water efficiency, daylighting and biophilia – the fundamental human need for the connection with nature. The building includes many passive design features that reduce energy consumption and increase user comfort. These include a large sunshade canopy over office and roof gardens, skylights allowing natural diffused light across the factory floor, concrete fins shielding against the low east and west sun and the forest to provide shade to the building and recreation space for building users.

Ecological aspects: natural light across factory floor and offices | floor slab varies between 25 mm to 200 mm thickness | roof 150 mm thick | rainwater harvesting | shading canopy | extensive greenery | double glazing to office | radiant slab cooling | off-form concrete: less material, reduced maintenance, structure acts as cooling element | production building is fully sealed and has fast closing loading bay doors | flexibility of column-free factory floors | magnetic bearing chillers | ventilation: DOAS energy recovery

Certificates / standards: Winner of WorldGBC Asia Pacific Leadership in Green Building Award, Commercial Building Category 2020

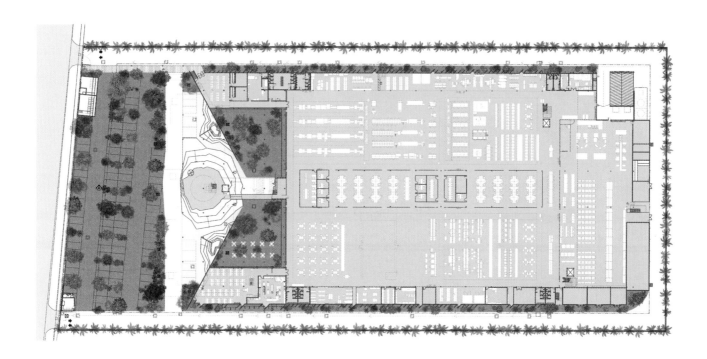

The building is designed to shield against the hot tropical sun, while allowing soft diffused natural daylight to filter into the building. The office and courtyard are shaded by a louver canopy designed to provide effective solar protection during the hottest part of the day. An innovative radiant floor cooling system cools down the slabs to about 21° Celsius using a high performance magnetic bearing chiller. This allows the more traditional air-con system to be significantly reduced thus saving energy. To alleviate flood risk from the tropical rainstorms, the building has an 800-cubic-meter stormwater retention tank as well as a 400-cubic-meter rainwater harvesting tank for landscape irrigation. Employees are working in an environment with diffused natural light throughout the day and a view to the sky. They are surrounded by greenery, with rainwater cascading from the roofs, shaded roof gardens and a courtyard to meet, relax and exercise in.

WELCOME TO THE JUNGLE HOUSE
CPLUSC ARCHITECTURAL WORKSHOP

Location: 59 Ivy Street, Darlington, NSW 2008, Australia | **Completion:** 2019 | **Client:** Clinton Cole & Hannelore Henning | **Landscape designer:** Bell Landscapes | **Building type:** residential | **GFA:** 185 m² | **Photos:** Murray Fredericks Studio / www.murrayfredericks.com.au

Welcome to the Jungle House (WTTJH) is a typology for future sustainable carbon neutral living. It is architecture that explores active and passive systems, the poetic, the emotional and the nurturing capacity of human beings to reverse the impact of climate change and to establish resilience through architectural design that addresses some of the profound pressures on the natural world. It is both a functional and a symbolic advocate for innovation design and sustainable living. It is architecture of climate change activism where sustainability, landscape, fauna and architecture exist symbiotically. The home is flexible for a growing family of five devoted to sustainability in all aspects of their lives; environmental, social and economic, without compromising the comforts and beauty that architecture offers. This project is about making the relationship between architecture and climate change reversal aspirational to the broader public. The 98-square-meter triangular site is situated in an inner-city Sydney heritage conservation area typified by late Victorian row terrace housing and post-industrial warehouses. Strict heritage controls restricted modifications to the existing spackled rendered façade.

Ecological aspects: solar power | wind power | roof: R 2.0 blanket foil insulation; clay beads and soil providing further insulation | wall(s): R 4.0 batt insulated exterior walls; R 2.5 batt insulated internal walls | floor(s): R 4.0 foam to underside of ground-floor concrete slab; R 3.5 to other floors | windows (Uw) U-value (average) of 5.0 | aquaponic system | rainwater collection | passive design strategies | 1600 l steel pond and 20 galvanized planter bed rooftop, braced to a steel and LVL structure | western red cedar windows and doors set within a masonry heritage façade | steel frame (long lifespan), clip system for PV façade (easy maintenance), home automation system, powered by solar energy

Certificates / standards: carbon neutral

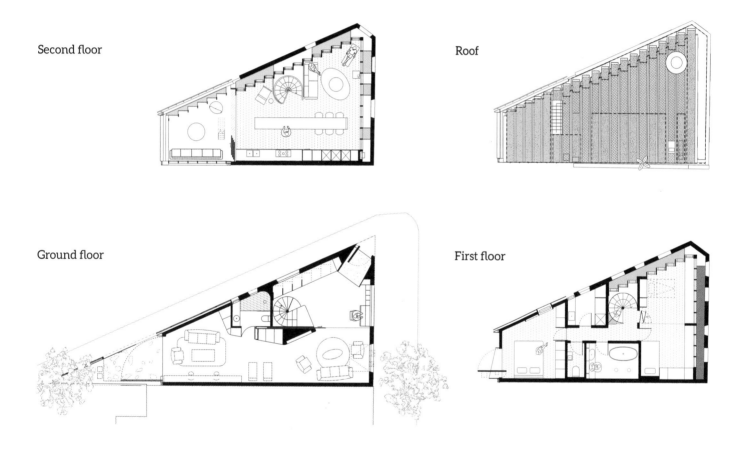

Second floor

Roof

Ground floor

First floor

What was initially presented as a challenge to retain the existing built fabric ultimately informed a dialogue between the old and the new, grounding the project within its urban context and becoming essential to the materiality, spatial and sustainability responses in the architecture. Acting as a beacon of sustainability where landscape, food, nature, garden, environment, energy, waste, water and architectural aesthetic exist in harmony, the house draws daily crowds from commuters and architecture students en-route from public transport hubs to the nearby University of Sydney. The concept was very deliberate in promoting integrated sustainability attributes into the façade and roof design on the basis of image-centric generations of students, architects, the public and more broadly, the global architectural community.

ECOCAPSULE
ECOCAPSULE LTD.

Location: anywhere | **Completion:** 2018 | **Original architect:** Tomáš Žáček, Soňa Pohlová, Matej Pospíšil | **Building type:** experimental | **GFA:** 8.2 m² | **Photos:** Katarína Selecká / www.katarinaselecka.com (21 b. r.), Adam Plesník / www.adamplesnik.com (21 a.), Tomáš Manina / www.tomasmanina.com (21 b. l.), CreaCrea Studio / www.creacreastudio.com (19 b.), vizualization (18, 19 a.)

Ecocapsule is a beautiful, smart, self-sustainable micro-unit, fully powered only by solar and wind energy, which charges the battery. Its uniqueness lies in its off-grid aspect, which means you can stay in remote places, or just anywhere completely without city infrastructure, with the luxury of a hotel room and its mobility. This micro-home is tailor-made to fit on the road, to be moved around on our customized trailer towed behind the car. It also perfectly fits into a standard shipping container so it can be shipped worldwide. Ecocapsule can stand freely as a cottage or a home-office on any piece of land, to be moved around on wheels mounted on the trailer, and also become a house-boat when placed onto our special certificated pontoon.

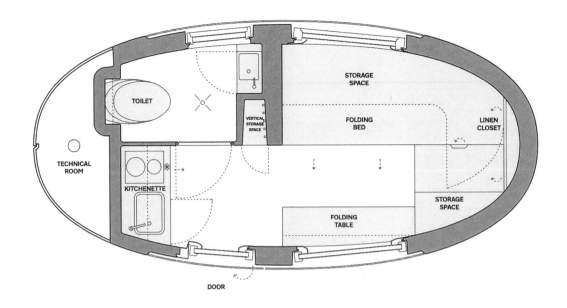

Ecological aspects: solar energy | wind energy | battery power storage | constructional, stainless steel | insulation through polyurethane foam and aerogel | lightweight plywood | glass | Polymethylmethacrylat | low styrene content resin | laminate | biodegradable oil | low maintenance structure and façade material lifespan up to 50 years | reuse possibility of insulation | composites and other materials | tanks for white, gray and black water

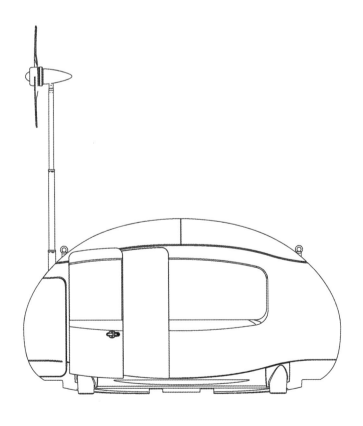

The idea to create a fully energetically independent micro-home was born in 2009, and today the first limited series of 50 is going to be sold out. Ecocapsule Ltd. have engineered the product from scratch and even waited a couple of years for the new technologies to make it as self-sufficient as possible. And the micro-unit is still improving. Systems of renewable energy and rainwater gathering are aspects that make the Ecocapsule sustainable and ecological. When Ecocapsule has enough solar and wind energy, and its users behave sustainably, it can be energetically fully self-sufficient. This presupposes that the user is aware of how much energy the capsule produced the previous day and use this supply effectively. This is actually perfect sustainability in practice – the owner will not be able to spend more energy than Ecocapsule produces from natural sources.

CITE DU VIN MUSEUM
XTU ARCHITECTS

Location: 134, quai de Bacalan, 33000 Bordeaux, France | **Completion:** 2017 | **Client:** Bordeaux Metropole | **Eco engineering:** Le Sommer Environnement | **Civil engineering:** SNC Lavalin | **Scenography:** Casson Mann | **Building type:** public | **GFA:** 14,800 m² | **Photos:** Julien Lanoo (22), P. Caumes (23), Anaka (24 a.), P. Tourneboeuf (24 b.)

The basic consideration that first came to mind when planning the Cite du Vin Museum was that the resulting building should reflect the spirit of the surrounding terrain. This place belongs to the river and the water is its life force. As the broad river winds gently, one of its curves forms the entrance to the port, the gateway to the city. The Cite du Vin Museum is a vertical icon on this horizontal skyline, a beacon that can be seen far and wide. It has a shape as smooth and rounded as a pebble. The building reflects the nature of the water surrounding it.

Ethereal, enigmatic, and atmospheric it looks like rising from the mists of the river. It is inspired by the spirit of the place, and dedicated to the spirit of wine. The building should correspond to a timeless manifestation of the essence of fluidity. In this regard, another concern was to illustrate the movement of the wine, its different fields and sectors inside and outside the building. In the interior, the visitors arrive at the forum by climbing the great staircase, curving gently upwards to the exhibition.

The visitors discover the exhibition, designed to evoke the idea of a whirlwind – like the movement which awakens a wine. The exhibition is thus laid out along a circular route and as an flowing space. The glass walls offer a spectacular view of the river. The outer shell of the building is characterized by the waves on the façade, the oscillating lines engraved on the glass, the glass cladding and the wooden structure. The wood used comes from sustainably managed forests. Other sustainable aspects of the building are the use of geothermal energy, geothermal heat pumps, the strong sealing and the natural ventilation.

Ecological aspects: heat network: biomass, geothermal energy, methanation | natural ventilation | geothermal heat pumps | wooden structure and frame | wood from sustainably managed forests | insulation: 25 cm of cellulose wadding | large exhibition space without pole, use is mutable

Certificates / standards: BREEAM Good | French Haute Qualité Environnementale (HQE)

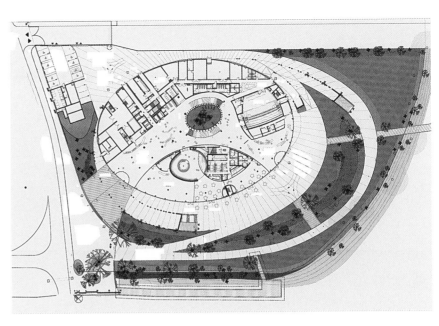

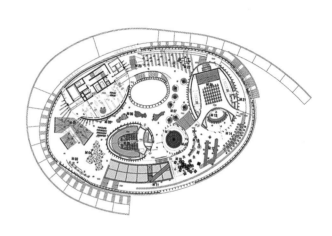

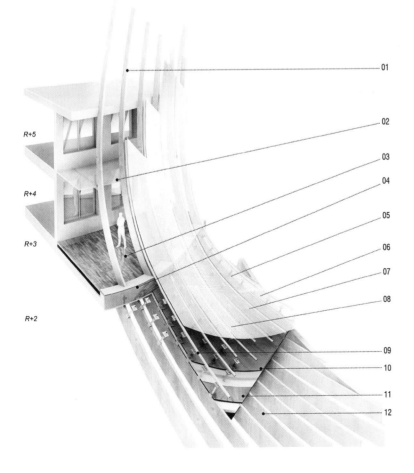

01 Exterior timber frame
02 Gratings
03 Slab on pedestals
04 Reference floor
05 Clear glazing
White dot enamel screen printing side 1
06 Gold hard coated glazing
07 Magnetron coated glazing
08 Hard-coated glazing
White dot enamel screen printing side 1
09 Fixture system of the cladding
10 Light gray membrane waterproofing
11 Organical-sourced insulation
12 Glued laminated timber arch

TREE SUKKASEM VILLA
TOUCH ARCHITECT

Location: Khaokho, Petchaboon, Thailand | **Completion:** 2013 | **Client:** Mr. P | **Original architect:** Setthakarn Yangderm, Parpis Leelaniramol | **Building type:** residential | **GFA:** 450 m² | **Photos:** Chalermwat Wongchompoo / www.sofography.com

The private residence, called Tree Sukkasem Villa, is located on the northern part of Thailand, approximately 1,200 meters above sea level. An outback terrain area with no electricity, water supply, or even other buildings nearby. There is only a native agricultural space. The concept of this house is to live without public electricity and water but with the house itself sustainable. In order to create green architecture, simple functions with clear design and easy to construct are the main points. The classic proportions of the building structure are reminiscent of the style of Mies van der Rohe. The simple style of the house is still comfortable because tropical design was added into the process.

Double walls and a concrete roof with wood trellis above help to reduce heat from natural sunlight. The cantilever roof also protects against hard raining and hailstone in rainy season.

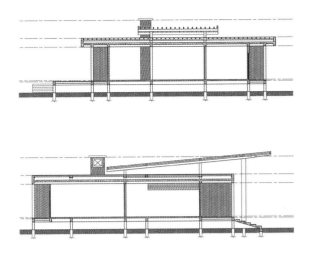

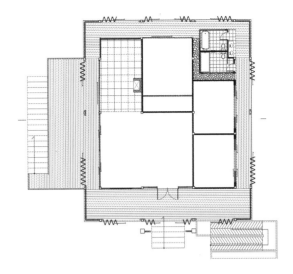

Clear glass windows allow natural wind ventilation, so there is no need for air-conditioning. The reinforced concrete roof was designed to use as a mini reservoir in order to collecting rainwater. The house was also built by using local materials. It integrates small vernacular with modern style, such as wood and bamboo from local bamboo trees, which can easily be found within this area or wood from old schools and other old houses. Moreover, diesel generator and solar panels were installed for producing electricity, while collecting rain and water from the mountains for water supply. 2 x 8 inches of the wood cladding on the wall can also be removed and used to repair the house in the future. It could be also reused as another house's structure.

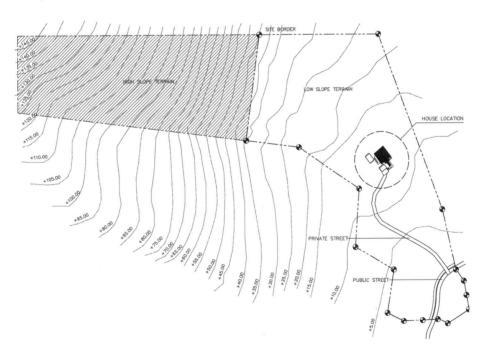

Ecological aspects: wind turbines | insulation by double walls and roof layer heat avoidance | natural ventilation | collecting rainwater | gravity mountain water | hard wood from old schools and houses | bamboo from local bamboo trees | reuse of gray water during construction

VIVIHOUSE
TECHNISCHE UNIVERSITÄT WIEN CEC

Location: Nordmanngasse 88, 1210 Vienna, Austria | **Completion:** 2020 | **Client:** TU Wien CEC | **Eco engineering:** Nikolas Kichler, Michael Fürst, Paul Adrian Schulz, Karin Stieldorf | **Building type:** residential | **GFA:** 137.5 m² | **Photos:** Robert Lichtveldt / www.lichtveldt.com

The vivihouse is a modular system with which up to six-story buildings can be realized in a collaborative and recyclable manner. The timber frame construction method was developed as part of a research project and is characterized by prefabrication, openness to use and non-destructive deconstructability. Against the background of the climate crisis and its urgency, vivihouse focuses on cooperation instead of competition and wants to enable planners to work together and learn from each other. This is reflected in the integrated open source idea, which allows individual elements to be worked on and further developed independently of each other. This allows vivihouse to be easily adapted to the cycle of local resources, building codes, production possibilities as well as design preferences.

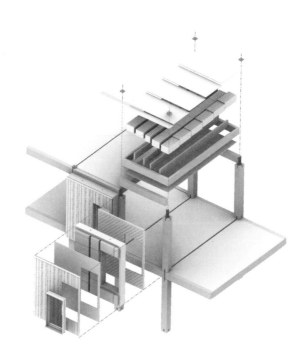

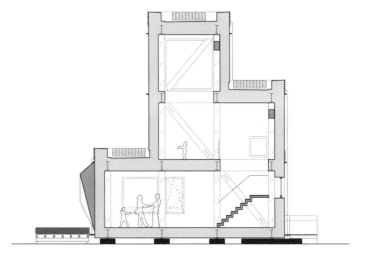

Ecological aspects: PV systems on all roofs | 0.13 W/m²K with 36 cm straw bale insulation | ventilation system with heat recovery | solar-optimized hot water boiler | solar-powered electric ceiling heating system | primarily renewable wood frame construction and straw bales | clay plasters and fill, no vapor retarders | green roofs | raised 30 cm on mobile concrete blocks | non-destructive demountable individual elements | façade independent of construction | low-wear steel nodes | skeleton construction for all kind of (re)uses | straw bales as insulation and main material with very low primary energy content (14 MJ/m³) | disposal indicator (EI10) of 8 | 38 kWh/m² energy certificate | CO_2 storage: balanced 15 t CO_2 equivalent greenhouse gas emissions

Certificates / standards:
Austrian Ökoindex 3 (OI3) of 399 Points

For example, a façade element could contribute to food or energy production. The three-story prototype was built by about a hundred students from the Vienna University of Technology and other interested laymen and laywomen in guided construction workshops. The materials used mainly include wood, straw bales and clay. The prototype shown here stands as a temporary building in the Donaufeld urban development area.

OASIA HOTEL DOWNTOWN
WOHA

Location: 100 Peck Seah Street, 079333, Singapore | **Completion:** 2016 | **Client:** Far East SOHO Pte Ltd | **Landscape design:** Sitetectonix Pte Ltd | **Building type:** mixed-use | **GFA:** 19,416 m² | **Photos:** Patrick Bingham-Hall / www.patrickbingham-hall.com (37), K. Kopter / www.kkopter.com.sg (34, 35)

A tower of green and red in the heart of Singapore's dense Central Business District, the Oasia Hotel Downtown is a prototype of land use intensification for the urban tropics. This tropical living tower incorporates plants into its red permeable aluminum façade and embodies multiple innovations in structure, organization, spaces, cladding and imagery. Offices, a hotel and club rooms are located on different strata, each with its own sky garden. These additional ground levels allow generous public areas for recreation and social interaction throughout the high-rise, despite the inner-city high-density location. They are open-sided for formal and visual transparency and allow breezes to pass through the building, making them functional, comfortable tropical spaces with greenery, natural light and fresh air. Landscaping is used extensively as an architectural surface treatment and forms a major part of the development's material palette, both internally and externally, achieving an overall Green Plot Ratio of over 1,000 percent.

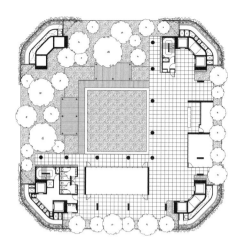

Plan sky terrace

Ecological aspects: sunshade | cross ventilation | daylighting – passive and intrinsic from the architectural massing and expression | extensive greenery lowers surface temperature | naturally ventilated common spaces reduce need for air-conditioning | planting attracts many species of animals, and brings biodiversity back into city | lush, living ecosystem by producing over 1,000 % of the greenery found on site prior to construction

Certificates / standards: Green Mark certified by the Building and Construction Authority of Singapore

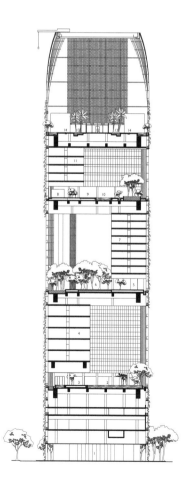

This quantum of green is an exciting number, as it effectively compensates for the lack of green in ten surrounding buildings. The tower's red aluminum mesh cladding is designed as a backdrop that reveals itself in between 21 different species of creepers, with colorful flowers interspersed among green leaves. It acts as a sun-shading skin that not only reduces the surface temperature of the building as well as the need for air-conditioning, but provides a safe haven for birds, butterflies and other animals, bringing biodiversity back into the city. The creepers form a mosaic with each type taking over its most suitable conditions of light, shade and wind. Instead of a flat roof, the skyscraper is crowned with a tropical bower; floral, diverse, soft and alive.

BAUGEMEINSCHAFT TEAM³
ARGE ARCHITEKTURWERKSTATT VALLENTIN
JOHANNES KAUFMANN ARCHITEKTUR

Location: Jörg-Hube-Straße, 81927 Munich, Germany | **Completion:** 2019 | **Client:** Baugemeinschaft Team³ | **Eco engineering:** Martin Such, Passivhaus Dienstleistung GmbH | **Landscape architects:** FreiRaumArchitekten GbR | **Building type:** residential | **GFA:** 4,430 m² | **Photos:** Lukas Vallentin / www.vallentin-architektur.de

The project is part of Munich's first ecological model house settlement. 488 residential units completely in wood and wood-hybrid construction. It is the largest wooden housing estate in Germany. The building community Team[3] is an amalgamation of the building community initiatives ArchitekturNatur, Holzbau findet Stadt and Wohnen ohne Auto. The ecological building in the ecological model settlement includes a mobility concept for car-reduced living with mobility stations, the installation of nesting boxes for building breeders and species protection, minimal surface sealing and a system for reusing rainwater. The varying and individualized floor plans of the 36 residential units range in size from 56 to 120 square meters. The site has three types of buildings, in a networked, dense development, which are connected by residential streets and alleys. The three-story community area in the south of the atrium house forms a meeting point and co-working space at the village square for communal activities of the residents. In the south, on the street, there are two compact four-story townhouses. As the tallest buildings they form the striking prelude to the construction site. There are two apartments each floor.

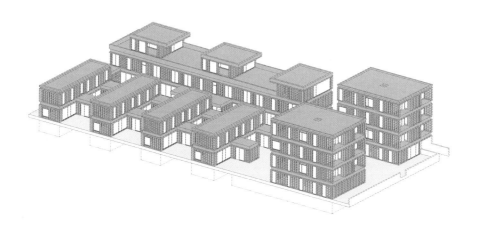

Ecological aspects: district heating: heat is distributed through a central pipe network in the basement | cellulose insulation with wood fiber insulation board | drinking water is prepared in central fresh water stations | the outer shells of all buildings are timber frame constructions, materials: spruce / fir, larch, pine / douglas fir, beech / oak / robinia, expanded cork, hemp / flat fleece

Certificates / standards: German Passivhaus standard with certificate

In the north, eight angular garden courtyard houses were built, in which a two-story main building and a single-story porch form a small garden courtyard. Ground-level glazing allows a connection to the own garden and the green roof area of the single-story porch. The garden courtyard houses are accompanied by a row of atriums, which, with two to three floors, form a border to the east. All roofs have gardens with terraces and raised beds that can be used by all residents. In general, intensive green-ing of the roofs and extensive infiltration of rainwater from paved areas in lateral green spaces ensure that as much rainwater as possible seeps away and evaporates in the root area of plants. High rates of evaporation are intended to alleviate the heat in the living environment at the height of summer. In this housing estate, the building consortium Team[3] took up the urban and landscape planning concept of an urban residential cluster surrounded by extensive parks.

POWER WING
OPENBOX ARCHITECTS AND OPENBOX GROUP

Location: 5 Krungthep Kreetha Road, Bangkok 10240, Thailand | **Completion:** 2020 | **Client:** B. Grimm Power | **MEP engineering:** Siam complete construction | **Consultant:** Solarcon | **Building type:** infrastructure | **GFA:** 1,211.10 m² | **Photos:** Panoramic Studio / www.panoramicstudio.myportfolio.com

After many successful design interventions of Openbox Architects and Openbox Group for large scale projects, the architects would like creating an awareness of the important of sustainable energy to public. The brief was to create an iconic piece of landmark at their headquarters office, that can send a strong message. B. Grimm Power is the leading professional firm in solar energy, the company's headquarters emphasis is using the solar panel and solar farm. The design integrates architecture with nature. The idea is to integrate other functions to keep the area alive, and take the opportunity to give something back – aside from clean energy – to the community. The design team studied the headquarters layout and proposed to create two multi-function objects at the office parking areas, at the most visible location from the main road. The architects realized a parking roof, completed with solar panels in a form of a stunning sculpture.

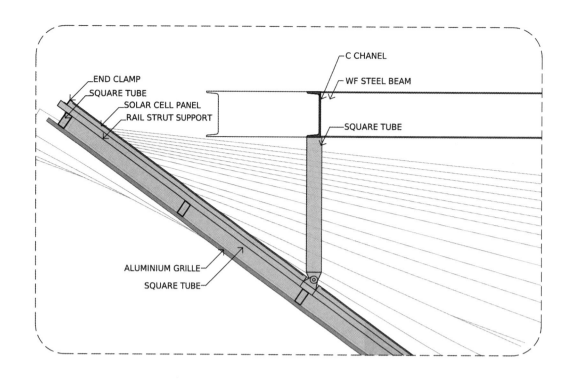

Ecological aspects: PV solar panel 390W measuring 1 x 2 m | 6 mm DC cable, AC cable-inverter unit 60 kWp, AC panel | smart logger

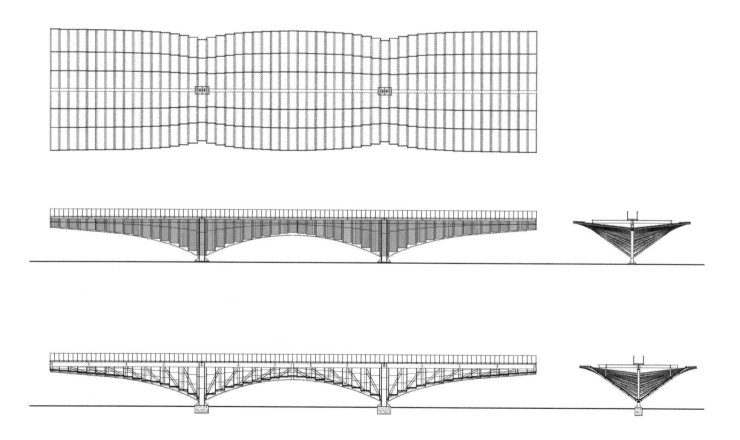

In order to create a more dynamic form, each solar panel was arranged in various angles according to energy waves to become the Power Wing. Also, it is inspired from B. Grimm corporate's value, the solar panel demonstrates the unity of people in their corporation. The piece of art itself will express engineering aesthetics by revealing a steel skeleton of a 50 meters piece of art with only two columns, and grand cantilever, combined with solar panels installations. This symbolized mankind's achievements in structural and energy engineering. Under the surface of the structure, are dashes of terracotta orange that stand for B. Grimm Power color identity. From the main street passing the front of the headquarters office and through the entrance road, the sculptures create a strong presence with the awareness as intended. More than just a visual landmark, the sculptures symbolize a connection between engineering and art, that should be perceived as one.

AKADEMIE AM CAMPUS KOTTENFORST
WAECHTER + WAECHTER ARCHITEKTEN

Location: In der Wehrhecke 1, 53125 Bonn-Röttgen, Germany | **Completion:** 2017 |
Client: Deutsche Gesellschaft für Internationale Zusammenarbeit (GIZ) GmbH, Bonn |
Construction partner: ap88 Architekten Part mbB, Heidelberg | **Structural engineer:**
merz kley partner GmbH, Dornbirn | **Building type:** education | **GFA:** 6,245 m² | **Photos:**
Thilo Ross / www.thiloross.de (46, 49 a., m.), merz kley partner GmbH, Dornbirn (48 a.),
Achim Birnbaum / www.achimbirnbaum.eu (49 b.)

The new building of the AIZ – Akademie der Deutschen Gesellschaft für Internationale Zusammenarbeit (short GIZ) – found its new location at the Campus Kottenforst near Bonn. Waechter and Waechter architects certainly set about planning a building that would create the ideal learning atmosphere. The structuralist design approach expresses the restlessness of learning – the constant searching, reflecting, rambling, the curious, looking in all directions, this despite everything disciplined and with systematic order. The building playfully fits into the building window and enters into a dialogue with the existing building through its diagonal position. The pavilion-like new building nestles into the landscape space of the adjacent Kottenforst and fits into the built, heterogeneous context in a small-scale and scaled manner. The triple-glazed transparent surfaces enable passive solar energy use. Vertical larch wood lamellas of the façade, supplemented by interior glare and sun protection curtains on the upper floor and exterior screens on the first floor ensure summer thermal protection. The main basis for the DGNB Gold Standard is increased energy efficiency and the associated low primary and final energy demand of the building.

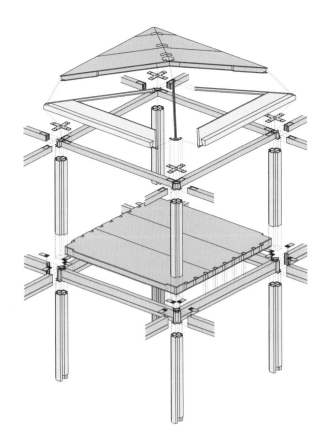

Together with the cluster-like and economically structured building design and the selection of resource-saving materials, the requirements for life cycle assessment and life cycle costs can be achieved. Environmentally compatible, pollutant-free materials are a prerequisite for improving indoor air quality. Particular attention was paid to limiting formaldehyde concentrations through the use of low-formaldehyde bonding of the wood box elements and formaldehyde-free tree-layer panels.

The building structure based on the wooden skeleton allows high variability and flexibility. This enables sustainable usability for the educational building, which can be well adapted to the future needs and necessities of educational and teaching concepts. The energy concept combines structural (passive) measures with an efficient plant technology consisting of block heating power plant and heat pump with geothermal probe field – seasonal pendulum storage – and absorption chiller.

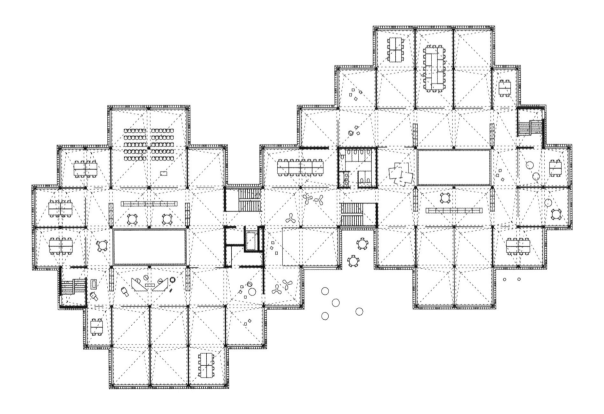

Ecological aspects: energy concept combines structural (passive) measures with efficient plant technology consisting of block heating/power plant and heat pump with geothermal probe field (seasonal pendulum storage) and absorption chiller | timber construction with environmentally friendly, pollutant-free materials | high flexibility and reusability, multi-modal learning landscape | module construction

Certificates / standards: DGNB standard Gold of the German Deutsche Gesellschaft für Nachhaltiges Bauen

SPIRAL GARDEN
RYUICHI ASHIZAWA
ARCHITECTS & ASSOCIATES

Location: Awaji City, Hyogo, Japan | **Completion:** 2018 | **Building type:** residential | **GFA:** 101.85 m² |
Photos: Kaori Ichikawa

The project is located on a 986.54-square-meter property on Awaji Island, Hyogo, Japan. To make the best use of the property, the house and its landscape were planned at the same time. The client, a family of four, explained that instead of a finished house, they wanted a house that they could finish themselves, a house that would grow with the family. The request prompted the office to rethink the ideal residence for the family. Various possibilities between the house and the garden emerged upon several studies. At the core of the house, there is an unassigned space, called

Niha. From the kitchen and dining room where the family would gather, the Niha is hidden from sight. During the day sunlight seeps through the skylight atop the Niha, with a diameter of 600 millimeters. At night darkness sinks as there are no lights installed. When opened, the skylight also functions as a tunnel to which the wind ascends from the ground.

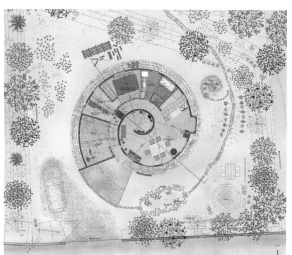

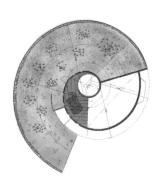

Ecological aspects: natural lighting due to special form of the house | regional wood and bamboo | traditional designs and production methods of the Awaji Island | regional soil | spiral roof as garden and habitat for different species of plants

As it is unassigned to a predefined function, the center of the house is free to be used for miscellaneous activities, be it meditation or gathering with friends. Its existence is significant in which it caters to the family's life dynamics. Although it is a peculiar form of architecture, the use of traditional wooden structures means that a lot of land is used to inherit the old-fashioned construction of private houses that remain on the island of Awaji. The spiral wooden structure hangs beams radially from the central cylindrical column and is exposed in the interior. Due to the shape of the roof and tri-directional curved surface, all elements were hand carved by a carpenter. The roof area was planned as a spiral garden, laid out by the owner, with ecology rising spirally from the ground. The spiral roof offers different orientations and heights from place to place and creates a habitat for a variety of different plant species depending on the sunlight and humidity.

CONCAVE ROOF SYSTEM
BMDESIGN STUDIOS, BABAK M. SADRI

Location: Jiroft, Kerman Province, Iran | **Completion:** ongoing | **Client:** confidential | **Sustainability consulting firm:** Nars | **Building type:** public | **GFA:** 772 m²

Concave roof system is a designed redundancy in the water supply. It efficiently harvests precipitation in the forms of rainwater and dew in hot and humid areas of southern Iran where the desert meets the Persian Gulf. Here humidity is high while there is a large temperature difference between day and night. Global warming is causing lower rainfall but higher relative humidity. On the one hand lower rainfall urge us to find newer methods for collecting it before it evaporates, and on the other hand, higher relative humidity indicates a higher opportunity for dew collection. Rain drops hit the earth at an incredible speed of ten meters per second and break up into droplets. In light rainfalls these droplets will eventually evaporate back to atmosphere while by employing a bowl shaped roof, these droplets will flow down, come together by a convergent slope and make bigger harvestable drops. This is exactly the same with dew collection. At night the cooling will lower the temperature of the micro-patterned polymer surface of the bowl-shaped roof, resulting the dew to appear in the morning or evening and flow down and harvested at the bottom.

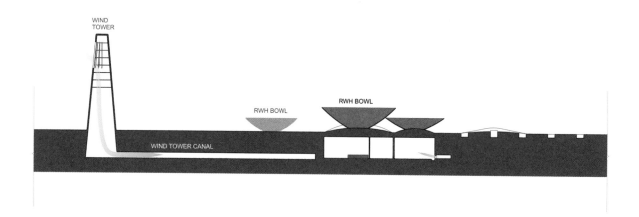

Ecological aspects: rain and dew harvest | adobe brick | micro-patterned polymer surface | very durable wooden structure and brick | incorporating water reservoirs in between building walls to benefit from heat storage capacity of water

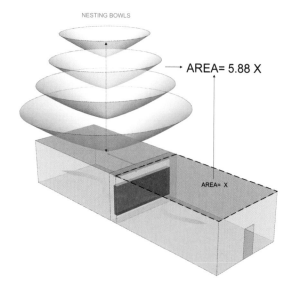

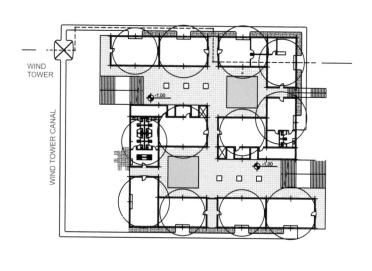

The outer bowl-shaped layer not only collects rainwater and dew. It also provides additional shading while allowing air to pass through the space between the bowls. This way it functions as a cooling mechanism for both roofs. The bowls themselves are nested, which provides 5.88 times more dew-harvesting surface for the bigger bowls and 4.12 times more, for the smaller ones. In this way, these nested concave roofs provides 3,601 square meters surface comparing to just 720 square meters if the roof was built conventionally. Connecting to the collection system, the reservoirs will be placed between building walls, to further control the temperature fluctuation of indoor spaces due to the heat storage capacity of water. This will lower the overall carbon footprint of much-needed air-conditioning. A wind tower is also designed for natural ventilation. This roof system will be beneficial for regions with low rainfall or high relative humidity with cold nights.

STADSKANTOOR VENLO
KRAAIJVANGER ARCHITECTS

Location: Hanzeplaats 1, 5912 AT Venlo, the Netherlands | **Completion:** 2016 | **Client:** Gemeente Venlo (Municipality of Venlo) | **Eco engineering:** Kraaijvanger in collaboration with C2C expolab | **Original architect:** Hans Goverde | **Building type:** public | **GFA:** 27,700 m² | **Photos:** Stijn Poelstra

The municipality of Venlo commissioned Kraaijvanger to design its new city hall. With 630 flexible workplaces and public functions, the building embodies the ambition to have the entire functions of city and region on the basis of Cradle-to-Cradle (C2C) principles. Basic C2C principles were lived up to: no fossil fuels are used, waste means food, create diversity. Well-being is the starting point and a good building makes people happier and boosts productivity. The spatial design is based on three goals. Firstly, bringing as much daylight and greenery into the interior as

possible. Secondly, creating routes through the building that stimulate people to move around. And finally, encounter others and use only healthy materials. The design includes an organic kitchen with a restaurant situated at the heart of the tower. Along with the spiral staircase system in the atrium, this encourages the use of the stairs. The parking garage with its green voids and building cooling system is the foundation on which the meeting functions are organized from the street level upward.

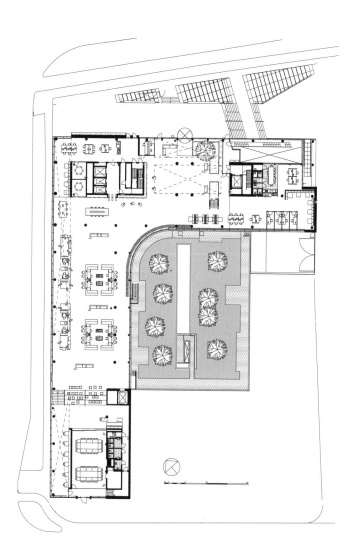

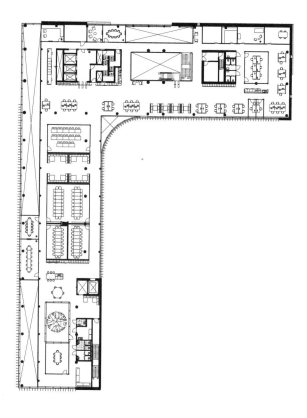

Ecological aspects: 1,500 m² PV panels | no gas | no fossil fuels | Resistance Class minimal 6.5 façades | triple glass | C2C circular products only | green lung façade purifies air via air transport system | building's green façade creates (bio)diversity | helophite pond recycles rainwater and wastewater | rainwater feeds green wall | passive ventilation chimney | thermal heath storage | earth cooling system | all materials C2C certified | no unhealthy materials or gas emissions | dismountable build for reuse | airtight, but users can overrule climate system to ventilate naturally | based on C2C principles | building is temporarily stack of raw materials | no waste | air quality and performance of users are monitored and investigated by university of Maastricht | sickness rate went down 2 %

Certificates / standards: C2C building

Around a patio with a helophyte filter for water purification, people can enjoy the greenery, the water and the views. Based on the open-house concept, which allows everyone to come and work in this part of the complex, the building connects people and staff. The offices are located on the floors above, in a secure zone in the tower. The complex comprises a single three-dimensional work environment: everything is connected to everything. The building refers to the agricultural tradition of this Limburg city and its top floor features a greenhouse with seasonal workplaces and room to grow regional products that also heats and humidifies the air that enters the building. The green air-purifying façade is the largest green building façade in the world and forms a protective shell against traffic and railway pollution. The glass window in the green façade offers a view into the heart of the building – the interior is visible from the inner city, in keeping with the transparency of democracy.

LOCHTEN HOUSING – A SUSTAINABLE MICRO-DISTRICT FOR ALL
URBAN PLATFORM ARCHITECTS

Location: Rue Van Hoorde, Rue Josaphat, Avenue Rogier, 1030 Brussels, Belgium |
Completion: 2019 | **Client:** JCX Immo | **Eco and technical engineering:** Matriciel |
Landscape architect: JNC International | **Building type:** residential | **GFA:** 6,222 m² |
Photos: Georges De Kinder / www.georgesdekinder.com

The Lochten Housing project's goal was to create a sustainable micro-neighborhood, integrating a mix of functions on a small area, in a dense urban zone. The interior area of the existing block includes 54 housing units of various type, common gardens and outdoor areas, a playground, collective spaces, a laundromat and space for various commercial enterprises and retail. The whole will essentially consist of a flexible, modular and repetitive construction system, based on a beam and column framework insulated with ecological cellulose fibers, and prefab wooden façades. Thanks to this system, around 20 percent of homes will meet the passive standard while the rest will fall into the low or very low energy category. Each building will be heated by an air-water heat pump with the back-up of a gas condensing boiler. Gardens in the ground as well as intensive and extensive green roofs, among others, ensure a good water balance. They also contribute to an important greening of the site and of the district as a whole. The project has permanently modified the ecological and social characteristics of the block which it has transformed. Numerous meeting spaces were created for the occupants of the site.

Ecological aspects: reuse of rainwater for common laundry | water management of landscape, ventilation double flux | heat pump | insulation made of cellulose in wooden boxes | prefab façades made of structural wooden boxes | removable façades and modulation for durability

Certificates / standards: contextual Passive House Planning Package | Belgian BatEx Exemplary Building

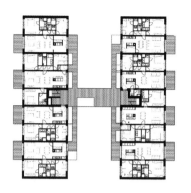

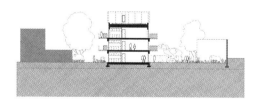

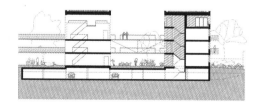

A small area playground for children, a vegetable garden with composting area, a communal garden and a terrace guarantee a quality outdoor setting. The maintenance of these collective places is envisaged through a form of participatory management, an organization very conducive to the accountability, social exchange and social control. The Lochten complex intends to play a leading role in the social dynamics of the neighborhood, in particular through the functional combination of various installations. Different activities – stores, offices, workshops – are established off-site around the residential blocks. Socially-oriented organizations, such as a health care center do also have their place. In collaboration with local actors, the investigators of the project create a carpentry workshop to offer new perspectives to young job seekers.

ORIENTATION
LUKE LOWINGS

Location: originally and temporarily in Hyllie, Malmö, Sweden; now relocated to Bergen, Norway |
Completion: 2017 | **Client:** Agrikultura – a triennial temporary group art exhibition | **Painter:** Marianne
Morild | **Fabricator / installer:** Montagegruppen, Malmö | **Building type:** temporary | **GFA:** 2 m² |
Photos: Peo Olsson / www.peoolsson.se, Luke Lowings (69 b. l.), Marianne Morild (69 b. r.)

Orientation – a Maquette for a Monument to the
Honeybee – refers to the extraordinary ability of
bees to find their way and communicate with reference to the position of the sun, and the damage
being done worldwide to these essential processes
by certain insecticides. A significant proportion of
human food is bee-pollinated; the sculpture serves
as a reminder of our conflicted relationship to the
rest of the natural world. The triangular monolith
has a brooding, enigmatic presence in the ambigu-
ous suburban landscape. Externally, images of bee
wings and flowers combine in dripping black gloss

oil paint – a reference to the petrochemical source
of the insecticide. Internally, the components of
bee orientation: geometry; gravity; the position
of the sun relative to the hive, are represented in
the form of a mysterious, dark hexagonal volume
with a glowing column of amber light at its center.
The column seems to emit six beams, only one of
which indicates the true direction of the sun.

Humans have become detached from specific landscapes, and most no longer identify with place in the direct, practical way that their ancestors did. For orientation they can rely only on relationships of culture and habit and the macro-natural world – weather, seasons, the sun itself. In an analogous way, bees can be moved as a community and re-orient themselves by the diurnal rhythm of the sun. Originally created for a temporary group exhibition on the edge of Malmö, Sweden, in 2017,

the work was acquired in 2018 for a sculpture trail in Bergen, Norway. A working beehive in the base of the structure is operated by local beekeepers. The materials used are timber, glass, acrylic and galvanized steel sheet. The project is estimated to have a lifespan of five to ten years, depending on the maintenance.

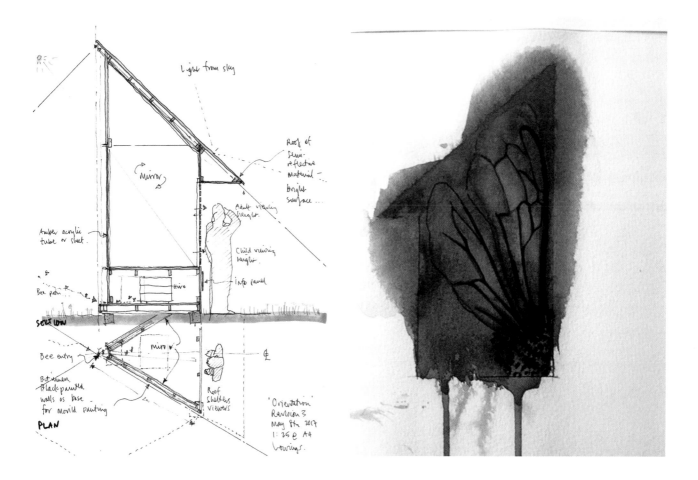

Ecological aspects: timber | glass | galvanized steel sheet | acrylic | temporary artwork | estimated lifespan 5–10 years depending on maintenance | incorporates bees from local beekeepers | requires community engagement

MFA NOORDERHUIS
DE ZWARTE HOND

Location: Noorderplein 2, 4225 RT Noordeloos, the Netherlands | **Completion:** 2019 | **Client:** Werkgroep Noorderhuis | **Eco engineering:** Merosch | **Building type:** mixed-use | **GFA:** 2,640 m² | **Photos:** Scagliola Brakkee / www.scagliolabrakkee.nl

In the Dutch village of Noordeloos, near the church tower, behind a row of trees stands the Noorderhuis. This consists of three smartly interwoven houses, which together form a building complex. The multi-functional accommodation (MFA) Noorderhuis accommodates a school, a gymnastics hall, a childcare center, a day nursery, a community center, a library and even a chapel of rest all under one roof, or rather three roofs. Due to the choice of materials and the sloping roofs the building is in keeping with the rest of the village and the rural surroundings. The community cen-

ter is a meeting point for the entire village, from young to old. The entrance is designed to stimulate interaction between indoors and outdoors. The windows and the roof lights ensure that the entire building has an abundance of natural light and a view of the surroundings.

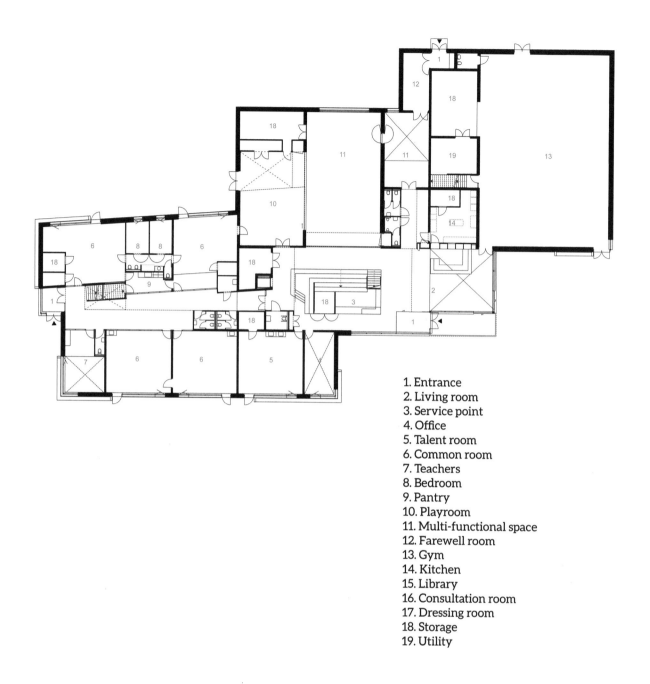

1. Entrance
2. Living room
3. Service point
4. Office
5. Talent room
6. Common room
7. Teachers
8. Bedroom
9. Pantry
10. Playroom
11. Multi-functional space
12. Farewell room
13. Gym
14. Kitchen
15. Library
16. Consultation room
17. Dressing room
18. Storage
19. Utility

Ecological aspects: 540 m² of solar panels | green roofs for insulation and water storage | heat-cold storage providing heating and cooling | larch wood from Siberia used | energy-efficient design | steel core can be disassembled over time

Certificates / standards: Dutch Energy Performance Coefficient EPC -0.019

The building is energy neutral, with an Energy Performance Coefficient of zero. Heat and cold storage provide heating and cooling in the building. A large part of the roof is covered with solar panels. The visible roofs are green and therefore good for insulation and water storage. The building has outstanding heat-cold storage insulation which provides the heating and cooling of the building and uses sustainable materials. Although the compact design of the building is energy efficient. The end result is a healthy, future-proof building with a comfortable indoor climate that all the inhabitants of Noordeloos can enjoy.

SHIRASU / SAKURAJIMA
ASEI ARCHITECTS

Location: Kagoshima City, Kagoshima Prefecture, Japan | **Completion:** 2019 | **Client:** confidential | **Building type:** residential | **GFA:** 202.88 m² | **Photos:** Daici Ano

The site is located in a residential neighborhood covering the hilltop overlooking Sakurajima. To the architects' surprise, an American owner asked for a sustainable residence using adobe or earth. He demanded for something like the architecture of a town like Taos Pueblo, an ancient village in the arid region of the United States designated a Unesco World Heritage Site. While using adobe bricks in Kagoshima was difficult due to its wet climate, the architects saw a primitive but progressive possibility in a house made with native soil. There is unused underground volcanic soil in Aira Caldera of Kagoshima known as "shirasu". Using shirasu, the architects designed a brick house that uses blocks as its foundational structure for the first time. With limited block and concrete aggregate resources in Japan, the architects put shirasu to practical use as an alternative source and proposed a new environmental architecture from a long-term perspective. They divided the masonry structure with limited allowance into small structures by room and arranged them in a way that allows the owner to explore their use.

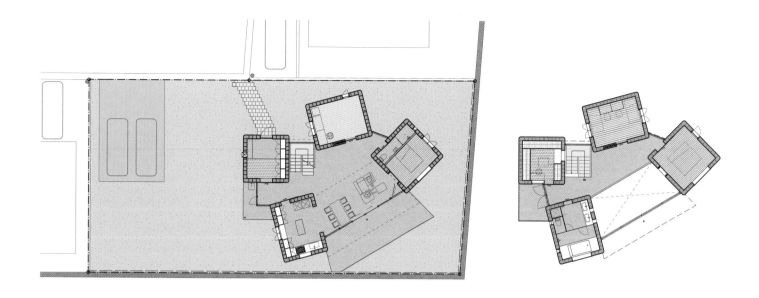

Ecological aspects: insulation and humidity control by masonry structure with shirasu block, made of recycled volcanic ash | heat storage by acquiring solar radiation on the inner wall | shirasu blocks are highly durable, have zero emissions and can be reused

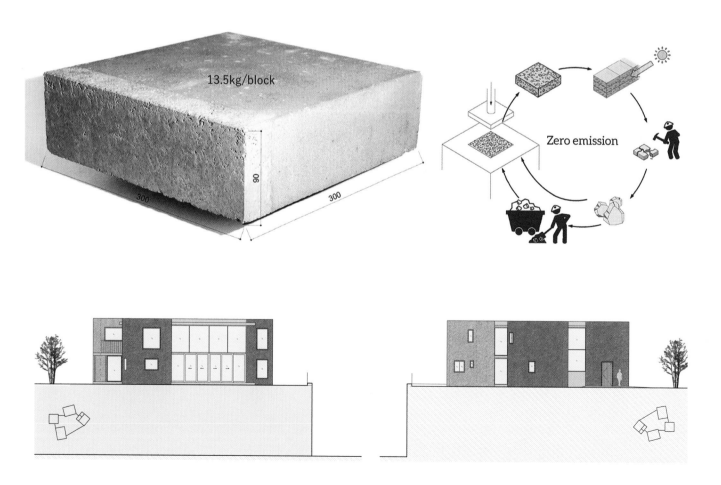

The space, that is full of possibilities, lets fresh air pass through in summer and retains heat in winter for comfortable indoor climate conditions, creating an atmosphere of a bright, sunny day. The balanced thermal environment achieved by the structure composed of shirasu blocks testifies the correlation between life and its surrounding. Therefore, the house allows the owner to connect with the natural world beyond the indoor situation and realize an open, relaxed lifestyle.

It is no exaggeration to say that this is just about the ideal integration of design, structure and equipment. With this house, the architects aimed for a new building style – structure based on regional characteristics – integrating design, structure and equipment, instead of retaining into materialism.

HIVE
OPENIDEAS ARCHITECTS

Location: Surat, Gujarat, India | **Completion:** 2019 | **Client:** K M | **Mechanical façade engineers:** Ensemble | **Building type:** residential | **GFA:** 600 m² | **Photos:** Panchkon / www.panchkon.com (79 a., 81 a.), Fabien Charuau / www.fabiencharuauphotography.com (78, 79 b., 81 b.)

Hive is conceived and designed as an intelligent, adaptable and sustainable family home at Surat, Gujarat. The form of the house is seeded in the profession of the client, who is part of an extremely successful company engaged in making machines for the diamond industry. The site is located in Vesu, an upcoming part of Surat. With the dominant presence of metal, the concepts of long span and light weight a complex form and fast construction came on board. The form itself was molded by an in-depth analysis of external temperature, humidity, solar radiation, cloud cover and wind pattern. The architecture is expressed as an angular V-shaped structure oriented towards the green pockets spread around the house. The entrance creates a bridge and valley experience, with a sunken court and stepped garden, a linear arrival corridor and the walkable green roof with varying slopes. This roof technically acts as a thermal insulation, lowering the overall temperature of the interiors, while functionally doubles up as a congregational area for social gatherings.

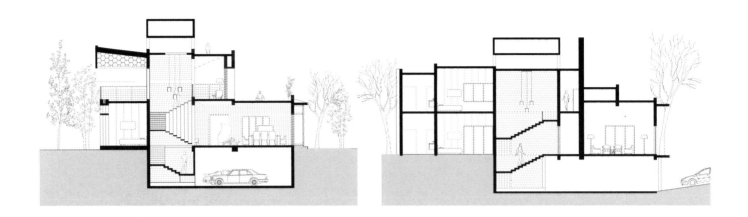

Ecological aspects: solar energy | wind energy | ventilation | rainwater harvesting | greening | green roof | longevity | adaptable | kinetic façade | energy saving | thermal comfort

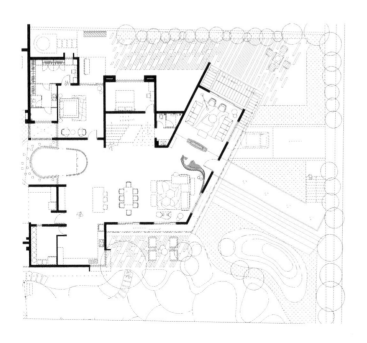

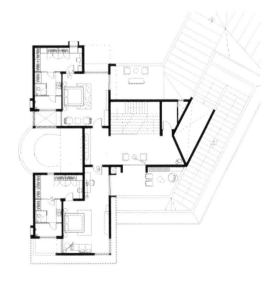

The architectural presence, undoubtedly, is established by the solar sensor-based façade, which lies at an exciting intersection of art and engineering. Its geometry is inspired by the hexagonal structural patterns found in nature such as those of honeycombs and carbon crystals, giving the project its name. Analyzed as per the structure, function and mechanism, its design is based on structural strength, transformability and biomimicry. The unique opening mechanism of the façade positions are derivatives of quality of light exposure and thermal comfort levels inside the house. Experientially, the modules create striking sciagraphy by casting patterns that change with the diurnal rhythm of the sun. The inspiration for the envelope and several other elements in the house, say the architects, were found in small, everyday things, for example the façade mechanism which was inspired by doors of airport buses.

GENOSSENSCHAFTLICHE
WOHNANLAGE WAGNISART
BOGEVISCHS BUERO
SHAG SCHINDLER HABLE ARCHITEKTEN

Location: Fritz-Winter-Straße 6–20, 80807 Munich, Germany | **Completion:** 2016 | **Client:** Wohnbaugenossenschaft wagnis eG | **Building type:** residential | **GFA:** 20,275 m² | **Photos:** Michael Heinrich / www.mhfa.de

The site lies like an island at the south-eastern end of the new neighborhood. The specifications of the development plan were limited to a circumferential building boundary and a maximum number of five stories. This provided the opportunity to freely form buildings that dialogue with the surrounding neighborhood through plazas and passageways while creating a place of community within. The group of buildings consists of five freestanding structures, named by the residents after the five continents, each of which fits around a central circulation core. The houses are linked to each other in recessed attics via bridges. This creates a roof garden landscape of unique size and diversity.

In addition to conventional apartments, new forms of living were also implemented, such as cluster apartments. On the first floor of the houses, a multitude of common rooms, studios, workshops and open spaces were created to serve the residents and, beyond that, the entire neighborhood.

One of the principles of the cooperative wagnis eG is participation – the involvement of residents in the planning process. According to jointly defined rules and regulations, design elements were developed by the future residents together with the architects. Central aspects for the community are the different areas in the open space. Courtyard spaces and interstitial spaces are used for arriving and meeting. Directly in front of the buildings, the open spaces were planned as an extension of the adjacent uses – as café terraces, as extended work areas in front of the studios and workshops, for lounging in front of the common rooms, and as vestibules in front of the building entrances.

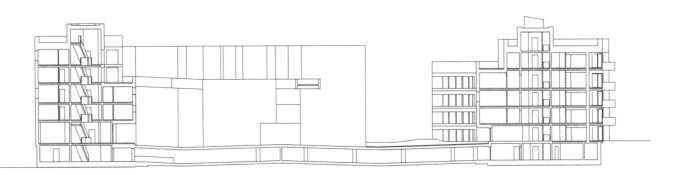

Ecological aspects: PV systems on three roofs | intensive green roofs / roof gardens | exterior walls non-load-bearing wood stud construction

Certificates / standards: German Passivhaus | German EnEV Energy Saving Ordinance

LIBRARY AT THE DOCK
CLARE DESIGN

Location: 107 Victoria Harbour Promenade, Docklands, Melbourne, 3008, Australia | **Completion:** 2014 |
Client: City of Melbourne, Places Victoria and Lend Lease | **Eco engineering:** Ché Wall with Lend Lease |
Building type: public | **GFA:** 3,038 m² | **Photos:** Dianna Snape

The Library at the Dock is part of the city of Melbourne's strategy of inserting libraries across the municipality. For Rob Adams, director of city design at city of Melbourne, each library is to be an urban exemplar, not just in terms of knitting together context, morphology and public space, but also in pushing the boundaries of technology, especially with regard to responsible environmental design. The library is a three-story lightweight timber building sitting atop the heritage dock structure. Architect of record was Hayball. Cross laminated timber technology is used for the upper floor slabs, roof, columns, beams and core wall construction. The height and placement of the building protects the new Buluk Park to the

south and a high north-facing porch, a gesture of welcome, echoes Melbourne's archetypal public signifier since the 1840s: the urban porch. The library is designed to offer 24-hour public access, multi-modal information and creative activities and promotes engagement with its context. As well as a traditional library collection, the library and community center offer an interactive learning environment and a state-of-the-art digital collection, multi-purpose community spaces, recording studio, music practice rooms and a performance venue that holds 120 people.

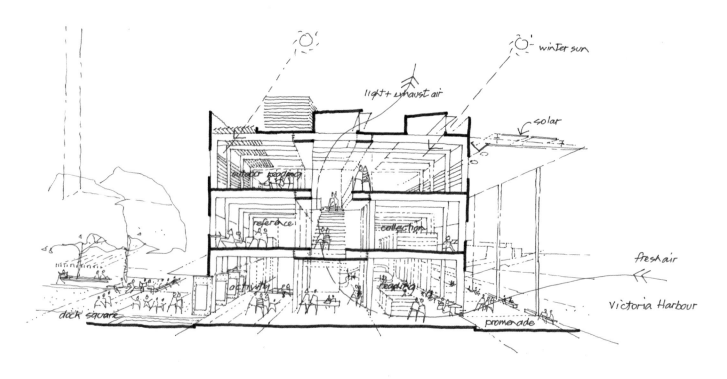

DOCKLANDS LIBRARY   CONCEPT SECTION.

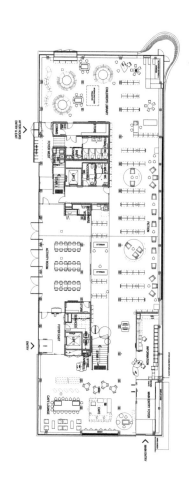

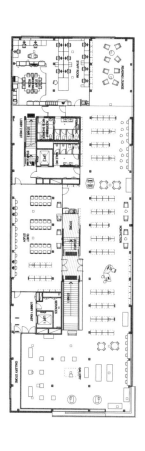

Ecological aspects: natural, passive ventilation system backed up with mechanical operable louvers on all four façades – to be opened in favorable conditions | in-slab hydraulic heating for ground floor | water harvesting from roof to a 55,000-liter tank for reuse | natural lighting | skylights also act as ventilation chimneys through stack effect | all furniture and fit-out selections contribute to 6 star Green Star rating | flexible planning arrangements | some areas can be fully opened to the outdoor spaces

Certificates / standards: 6 star Green Star for Public Buildings

Connection to Docklands' maritime and Aboriginal heritage is embraced and celebrated with facilities to support local historical research and educational experiences. Environmental achievements include carbon neutrality and optimized passive environmental systems. The library has become Australia's first 6 star Green Star public building. The design seeks to moderate the placeless world of electronic data by fostering comfort, identity and engagement.

CHOCOLAB + CHOCOHABS
MEC ARCHITECTURE

Location: Necoclí, Antioquia, Colombia | **Completion:** 2019 | **Client:** Casa Luker S.A. | **Building type:** residential | **GFA:** 404 m² | **Photos:** Luker Chocolate (91 b.), Manuela Eblé Cardenas

Chocolab + Chocohabs is a project for development and innovation whose main objective is to stimulate cultural and knowledge exchange that promote social transformation and sustainability. The project itself is an example of what is achievable with local materials and technologies that respond efficiently to the environment. The design of the building is based on passive strategies that reduce energy consumption throughout the life cycle of the building. The project actively involves the community in the construction process; it serves as an educational program on the trans-

formation and use of wood. The building seeks to give a new meaning to traditional local construction and serves as a location that the community can embrace as its own. The primary objective of the project was to provide the community a space with the lowest possible environmental impact. The first consideration was to use wood, which is a material found on site. This very sustainable material does not only reduce the carbon footprint on itself, but also because it does not need to be transported.

Ecological aspects: natural ventilation | natural illumination | rainwater use | locally-sourced wood from teak and melina tree | dry toilets that use cocoa husk and sawdust to transform solid waste into compost: later used in the cocoa farm | implementation of non-chemical soap use | water treatment is managed through a simple septic well and infiltration field

Furthermore, the architects considered passive strategies to ensure thermal comfort like natural lighting and ventilation so that they could reduce the use of energy of the building. In addition, they implemented the use of recollected and treated rainwater as the primary and only source of water in the building and during its construction. Finally, the architects opted on treating the wood with natural products as opposed to polluting chemicals. Chocolab allows a flexible use of interior space, divisible into two or three different spaces for different activities, also with possibility of opening to the exterior and expanding the floor area. Chocohabs has two sleeping areas that can easily be transformed into one big area by removing a single wood wall.

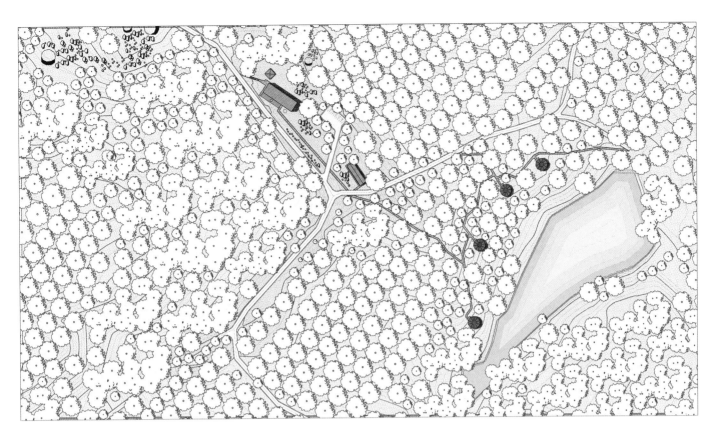

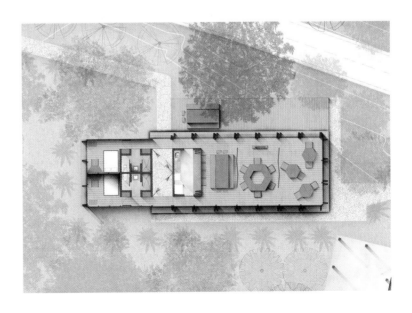

ROBUSTES WOHNEN AM PARK
ZILLERPLUS ARCHITEKTEN UND STADTPLANER

Location: Norbert-Glanzberg-Straße 2 and 4, 97074 Würzburg, Germany | **Completion:** 2020 | **Client:** GBI Wohnungsbau GmbH & Co. KG, Erlangen | **Eco engineering:** bauart Konstruktions GmbH & Co. KG | **Landscape architects:** fischer heumann landschaftsarchitekten PartG mbB | **Building type:** residential | **GFA:** 2,636 m² | **Photos:** Florian Holzherr / www.florian-holzherr.com

On the edge of the park at Hubland in Würzburg zillerplus architects and urban planners designed the project with the translated name Robust Living at the Park. In this new building complex from 2020, it is possible to live urban and yet pleasantly surrounded by greenery. The robust structures of the two wooden buildings of the residential complex are smoothly adapted to the climate. In record time, the two houses with mirror-image floor plans were each built around a staircase core made of reinforced concrete in the timber element construction of wall and ceiling panels both quickly, as well as resource and CO_2 low and efficient. The construction form of the houses has a relatively small surface area in relation to the volume, so that cold or heat can affect them only slightly. Solar control glazing and curtains provide additional protection against excessive heating.

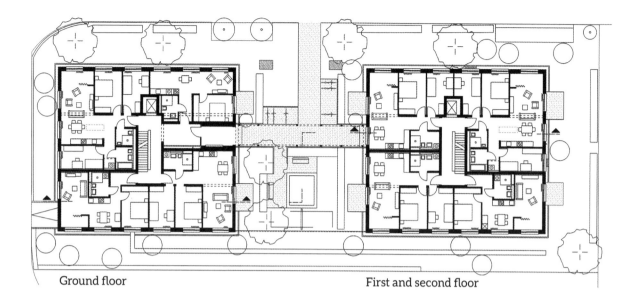

Ground floor   First and second floor

Ecological aspects: mineral insulation | renewable wood | robust construction and design | optimized surface-area-to-volume ratio | warm winter gardens as buffer space | compact light-flooded floor plans | high degree of prefabrication

Certificates / standards: German KfW 55 standard

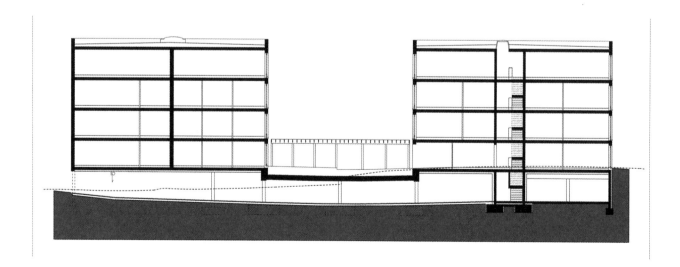

At the same time, the residential layout, with four apartments on each stairwell corridor, creates an intensive neighborhood. Freely financed and subsidized apartments are mixed horizontally in the house. Due to the compact design of the houses, all apartments have sufficient depth to accommodate kitchens and bathrooms in their center. Floor-to-ceiling windows direct pleasant daylight into their centers. An integrated warm winter garden with particularly large opening sashes can be used as a loggia or room in a climatic buffer zone. In front of and between the buildings, open green spaces and children's playgrounds have also been integrated. Thus, family-friendly and nature-oriented, but above all energy-saving living is possible here.

SOLAR FITNESS & WELLNESS UNIT NEST
DRANSFELDARCHITEKTEN

Location: Empa, Überlandstrasse 129, 8600 Dübendorf, Switzerland | **Completion:** 2017 | **Client:** Empa Swiss Federal Laboratories for Materials Science and Technology | **Eco engineering:** Naef Energietechnik, Miloni Solar | **Building type:** experimental | **GFA:** 250 m² | **Photos:** Zooey Braun (98), Reinhard Zimmermann

On the site of the Empa research institute in Dübendorf, an experimental building is growing that demonstrates innovative development in building by means of different units. One of these units, the Solar Fitness and Wellness Unit, serving recreation and health, has accomplished both an unusual energy efficiency and a convincing architectural solution. At the heart of the project are three floating ellipsoids, each containing a wellness module. These are accessed via walkways. A zero-energy balance is achieved through photovoltaics and solar thermal energy. Temperatures of up to 120° Celsius are generated by a CO_2 heat pump, which provides heat for the sauna and the steam bath reaching an efficiency three times higher than conventional systems. This enables it to replace over 60 percent of the electrical energy required for wellness facilities with environmental heat. A newly designed heat dissipation and steam generation system allows the use of heat above 100° Celsius. Both the roof and the façade are optimized for energy recovery. Further savings are possible through optimized insulation and ventilation with heat and moisture recovery.

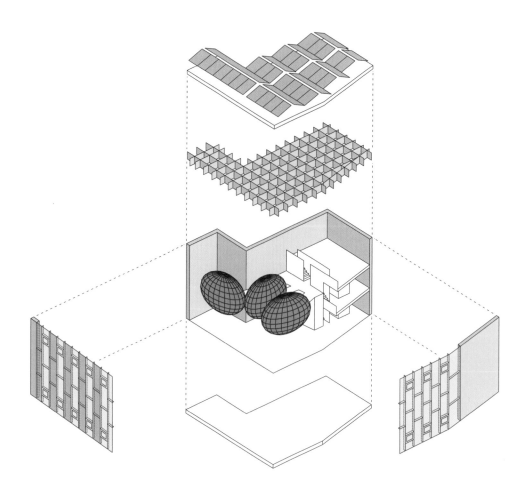

Ecological aspects: geothermal | solar thermal | PV | electricity from veloergometer | insulation: rock wool; insulating glazing 3- to 4-fold | CO_2–heat pump (flow up to 120° C) | ventilation with heat recovery | wooden element construction | three months construction time in existing structure (backbone)

Certificates / standards: zero-energy sauna

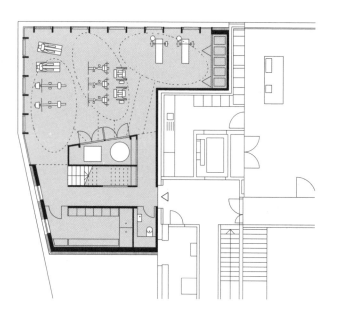

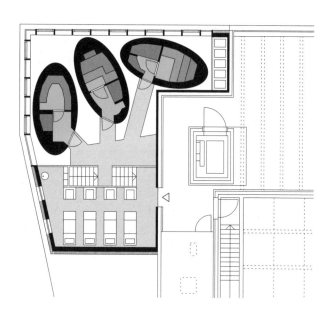

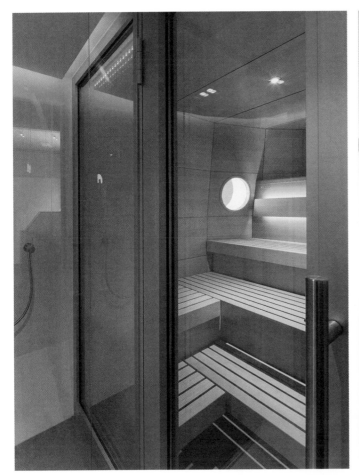

Saunas and steam baths can thus be operated with solar energy in an environmentally neutral way. Generating electricity by home trainer and a wellness area powered by solar energy: With the solar fitness and wellness facility, NEST shows that these needs can also be met sustainably – and at the same time promotes the health and quality of life of the users. Densified construction in cities often requires maximum utilization of the northern façades. How do you realize a transparent, com-fortable and energy-efficient north façade? Here, an eight-meter-high four-fold glazing is tested on the north side of the Fitness and Wellness Unit. With an insulation value U of 0.3 W/(m²K), this façade achieves a more favorable thermal balance in the winter half-year than a highly insulated wall five times thicker, while at the same time providing a high level of comfort and daylight.

ASHEN CABIN
HANNAH, LESLIE LOK AND SASA ZIVKOVIC

Location: Ithaca, NY, USA | **Completion:** 2019 | **Client:** confidential | **Building type:** residential | **Site size:** 100 m² | **GFA:** 10 m² | **Photos:** Andy Chen

Ashen Cabin is a small building 3D-printed from concrete and clothed in a robotically fabricated envelope made of irregular ash wood logs. From the ground up, digital design and fabrication technologies are intrinsic to the making of this architectural prototype, facilitating fundamentally new material methods, tectonic articulations, forms of construction, and architectural design languages. The cabin has a footprint of three by three meters and lifts off the ground on 3D-printed legs which adjust to the sloped terrain. All concrete components for the project were fabricated on a self-built large-scale 3D printer using a custom 3D printing process and utilizing corbeling as a design strategy. The concrete structure is characterized by three programmatic areas, a table, a storage seat element, and a 6.5 meters tall working fireplace. Ashen Cabin challenges preconceived notions about material standards in wood. The cabin utilizes wood infested by the Emerald Ash Borer for its envelope which is widely considered as waste.

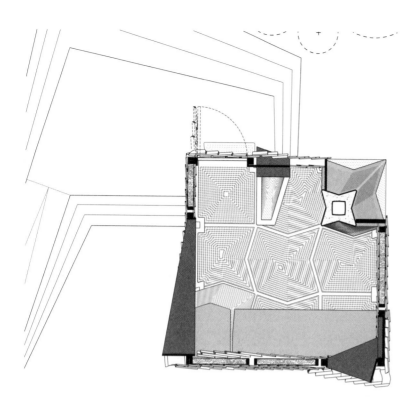

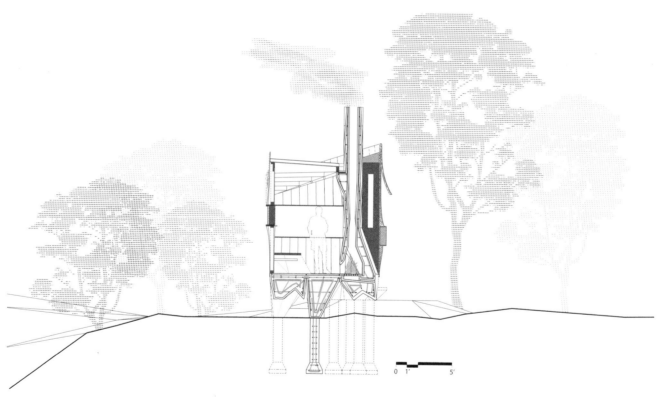

Ecological aspects: robotic fabrication increases efficiency and helps reduce waste material | use of Emerald-Ash-Borer-infested wood for construction purposes | upcycling of infested timber | concrete 3D printing eliminates the need for formwork | reduction of concrete waste through 3D printing

Due to their challenging geometries, most infested ash trees cannot be processed by regular sawmills and are therefore regarded as unsuitable for construction. Ashen Cabin presents a pathway to address the massive environmental problem caused by the Emerald Ash Borer in North American forests. By implementing high precision 3D scanning and robotic based fabrication technology, the architects of Hannah upcycle Emerald-Ash-Borer-infested waste wood into an abundantly available, affordable, and sustainable building material. The façade assembly is fully ventilated, detailed to manage shrinkage and does not require an additional rain screen. Irregular tree logs are robotically sawn into naturally curved boards which are then arrayed into interlocking SIP façade panels, Structural Insulated Panels. While transformed, the natural tree remains legible in the design.

FORSYNING HELSINGØR
CHRISTENSEN & CO ARCHITECTS

Location: Energivej 25, 3000 Helsingør, Denmark | **Completion:** 2018 | **Client:** Helsingør Supply & Administration | **Eco enineering:** Moe consulting engineers | **Landscape architects:** Third Nature | **Building type:** office | **GFA:** 6,000 m^2 | **Photos:** Niels Nygaard

With its five floors and 24 meters in height, square shape and rusty red façade, the main building of Forsyning Helsingør's – Helsingør Utility – new operations center is in architectural dialogue with the area's other large, geometric buildings. Sharp and sculptural, the building establishes a strong and characteristic appearance experienced both from the outside, from above, and from great distance. Inside, however, the cube is an open and honest building that generously displays its, at once, beautiful and raw interior. When customers and guests enter the power plant's new headquarters, they are greeted by a great view of the double-high reception area with a view up through the bright atrium, where the light falls from the

skylights. From the ground floor, you can overlook the entire organization in one glance – from reception to lounge area and further up to the open office landscapes in the upper part of the building. The building's façade is designed to utilize daylight in an efficient and sustainable manner. Its architectural layout and design ensures optimal supply of daylight via its atrium and façade, whose stationary shutters have the right degree of opening in relation to light and heat.

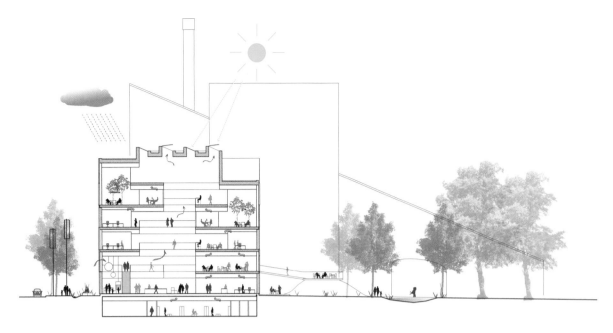

Competition proposal

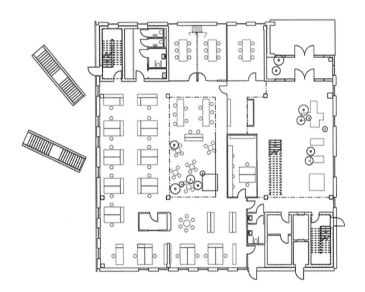
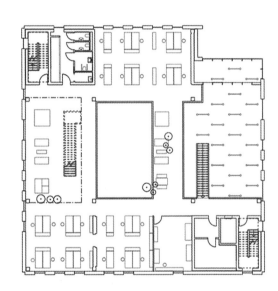

Ecological aspects: heat from a nearby wood-chipping plant | rainwater collection from surrounding areas | roof holds solar panels | optimal insulation | low energy windows | energy-efficient ventilation system | building materials of great quality and environmental profile | CO_2 footprint kept as low as possible | building's façade design utilizes daylight efficiently and sustainable

Certificates / standards: Danish Energy Rating A 2020

From top to toe the cube is covered with five milimeters thick corten steel plates. A robust material, not vulnerable to dirt, whose warm reddish-brown color contrasts well with the building's more technological aesthetics. The entire operations center has a both aesthetically beautiful, modern and technical design, where the technique is visible and stands completely raw. The new combined operations center unites the extroverted customer and learning functions with Forsyn-ing Helsingør's operational and administrative work. Herein lies the foundation of an open and vibrant inner universe, where a common team spirit across professionalism and job function can thrive and be instrumental in an equally open and vibrant corporate identity. Not all the solutions of the competition proposal have been incorporated in the final project.

PRVOK
SCOOLPT

Location: Vltava River Prague, Czech Republic | **Completion:** 2020 | **Client:** Stavební spořitelna Buřinka | **Landscape architects:** Envilope | **Eco engineering:** Jiří Vele, Kateřina Nováková | **Original architect / sculptor:** Michal Trpák | **Building type:** experimental | **GFA:** 43 m² | **Photos:** David Veis, Fox Art / www.foxart.agency

The original and unique floating livable sculpture 3D-printed from concrete is named Prvok. It combines art and architecture with innovation and 3D printing. This new technique enables architects to easily prototype buildings without producing much waste. It has a very modern look as well, showing that this new kind of technique might lead to a different future. The 3D printing look is repeated in the bathroom, while on the outside a greened wall and the green roof offer different surfaces. This original, the Prague-based prototype, will lead to the development of other buildings and forwards the evolution of visuality and form of housing. It is the first 3D-printed floating building in the world, inspired by nature, designed by a sculptor in collaboration with architects. The design and artistic attitude is linked to a function and its transportability.

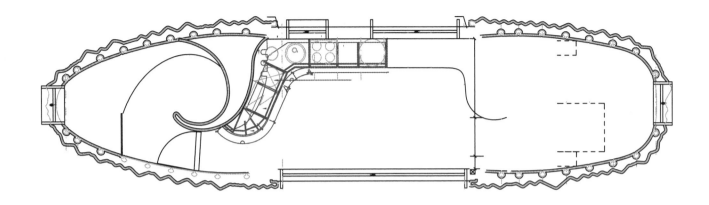

Ecological aspects: recirculating shower | insulation through sprayed foam | divided gray and black water systems | recuperating ventilation | green roof and walls | recycled 3D-printed PET products for interior | long-lasting structure | possibility to recycle at the end of lifetime

Certificates / standards: very low energy consumption

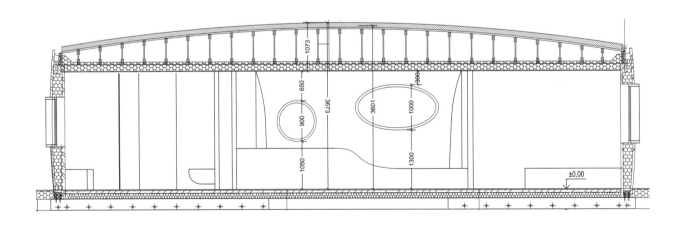

Prvok is equipped with two sources of heat: electrical floor heating and an air-conditioning unit connected to an air-air (water) heat pump, which conducts even recuperation of the inner environment. A mobile application enables the user to set the temperature of the indoor room. There is a unique system of touch switches which measures both temperature and humidity of the inner environment. Besides the settings On and Off the switches do handle various light scenarios.

One switch handles more light sources only by the number of touches due to an application. Prvok measures the total consumption of drinking water and – in case it's connected to containers – even the level of waste liquid: gray and black water. Thanks to a smart system of the shower, based on recirculation, Prvok is able to save water.

KRUSHI BHAWAN
STUDIO LOTUS

Location: Unit 4, Keshari Nagar, Bhubaneswar, Odisha – 01, India | **Completion:** 2018 | **Client:** State Government of Odisha, Department of Agriculture & Farmers' Empowerment | **Landscape consultants:** ROHA Landscape Architects | **Crafted jaalis & folk art:** Collective Craft | **Building type:** office | **GFA:** 12,077.40 m² | **Photos:** Sergio Ghetti (116 b.), Noughts & Crosses LLP and André J. Fanthome

Krushi Bhawan is a facility developed for Government of Odisha's Department of Agriculture and Farmers' Empowerment. The administrative center has been designed as an office for a team of nearly 600 people, in addition to accommodating spaces for community engagement and learning. Krushi Bhawan is located in Bhubaneswar, the state capital of Odisha. Home to multiple agrarian communities, the state is the third largest contributor to India's grain supply. Indigenous passive design strategies contribute to the sustainability parameters of the building. The courtyard morphology and the inclusion of a stilt level aid optimal air circulation through the building, whereas the low window-to-wall ratio and deeply recessed windows and balconies help lower heat gain. The building profile along the Central Court is characterized by staggered masses which enables self-shading and blocks direct glare. The use of locally-sourced materials has also lowered the carbon footprint of the construction process. The façade has been designed to ensure 100 percent daylit internal spaces.

Ecological aspects: building employs roof-mounted solar panels | façade designed to ensure 100 % daylight internal spaces | low window-to-wall ratio and deeply recessed windows and balconies lower heat gain | double-skin façade strategy – Double Glazed Units – reduces heat gain to 40 % by regulating ingress of sunlight | reduction of temperatures by 7–8° C through night ventilation system | air-conditioning via HVAC systems | on-site rainwater harvesting and wastewater treatment | anaerobic bio-digestive solid waste management system generates compost and fertigation water for the landscape | primarily locally-sourced materials, including laterite and khondalite, reducing the building's carbon footprint | regional crafts

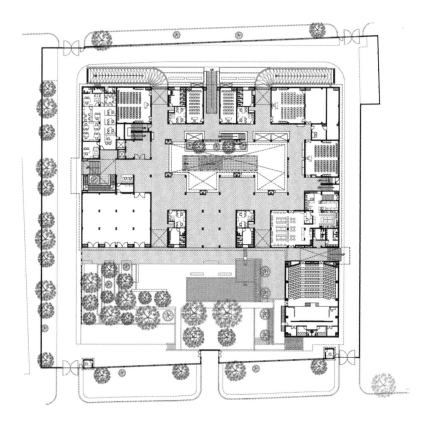

Further, a double-skin façade strategy has been put in place at the complex, which consists of double glazed units (DGU) on all external fenestration with louvers. Sill projections act as shading devices. A system that reduces heat gain to 40 percent by regulating ingress of sunlit. Bhubaneswar experiences significant drops in night temperatures through the year. Taking this into consideration, a simple night ventilation system has been devised for cooling and ventilation. Through this mecha-

nism, cool air gets pulled into the building through the northern façade when temperatures drop at night, by means of a custom-designed low-tech damper system. Other interventions include solar panels on the terrace, on-site rainwater harvesting and wastewater treatment, and an anaerobic bio-digestive solid waste management system which generates compost and fertigation water for the landscape.

MARINE EDUCATION CENTER
NORD ARCHITECTS

Location: Ribersborgsstigen 4, 21613 Malmö, Sweden | **Completion:** 2018 |
Client: City of Malmö | **Building type:** education | **GFA:** 700 m² | **Photos:** Adam Mørk /
www.adammork.dk

The Marine Education Center in Malmö is a new learning landscape that explores the effects of climate change and promotes sustainable development by the sea. Under a huge roof, where landscape and building become one, visitors can learn about sustainability and peoples' impact on the marine life. Back in 2014 NORD Architects won the competition for a new Marine Education Center in Malmö, Sweden, with an iconic building that engages visitors through hands-on experiences with life in sea and sustainability. The new center blurs the distinction between architecture and landscape and creates a smooth transition from coast to sea. The Marine Education Center's goal is to improve marine conditions by promoting the knowledge, awareness and responsibility of citizens, business and decision-makers. The building wants to welcome everyone from school groups to families. Flexible learning spaces lie under the unifying roof, creating an environment that accommodates both indoor and outdoor activities and encourages visitors to dive into a multitude of experiments and explore scientific knowledge with a focus on marine life. The building itself was designed to promote a sustainable approach and the roof expresses a performative combination of sustainable concepts and techniques.

All technical installations – including water handling and circulation, ventilation, solar energy production and consumption – were all on display in the competition proposal and meant to form an integral part of the entire learning experience on resources and sustainability. Johannes Molander Pedersen, partner at NORD Architects said it was important to develop a learning landscape where education is everywhere. It is in the landscape, in the building and in the transition between nature and culture. The center is open for everyone who is interested in the role we as humans play in nature's life cycle. It provides a hands-on learning experience that invites users to explore using their senses in the field, and thereafter analyze and understand their observations of the marine life.

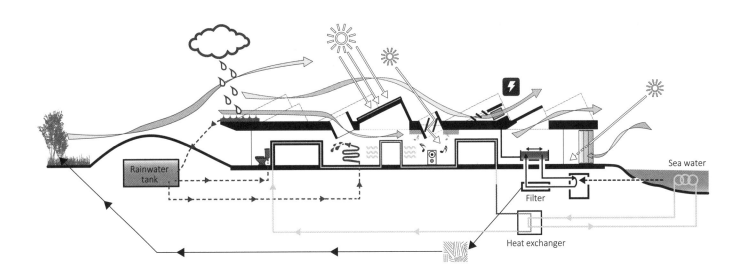

THE MODERN VILLAGE OFFICE
ALPES GREEN DESIGN & BUILD

Location: 01 Tran Duy Chien Street, 550000, Da Nang, Vietnam | **Completion:** 2017 | **Client:** Alpes Green Design & Build | **Original architect:** Ho Khue | **Building type:** office | **GFA:** 350 m² | **Photos:** Hiroyuki Oki

The Modern Village Office is an example of how a group of young professional architects invest in a low-budget project. They were eager to have a comfortable and local workplace for themselves, the members of the team and other enthusiasts. Therefore, the construction cost factor was the main priority. Thus, no professional construction contractors were hired. Mainly local labors, even friends and family members who were unemployed also participated in the construction process. In order to achieve good quality, a construction engineer was in charge to manage this process, to lead the works and to monitor all construction tasks. Main materials and finishes were carefully studied and designed to have an optimal solution in terms of price and to ensure the main idea all the way through. An artistic combination of elements harmonizes with the building.

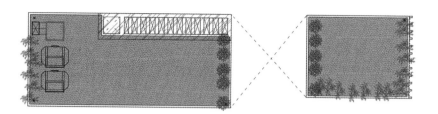

Ecological aspects: use of concrete slab system, enhanced with green plating creates effective insulation | natural instead of mechanical ventilation | natural light instead of lightning systems | reducing impact of the works to nature by reusing native trees on the site | roof covered with plants and trees to reduce heat of the interiors

Certificates / standards: Lotus Silver of the Vietnam Green Building Council (VGBC)

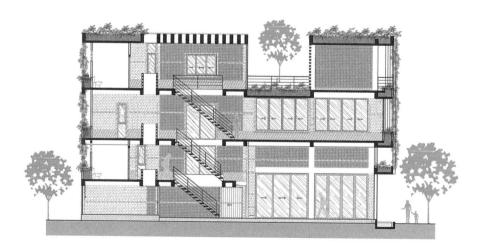

The Modern Village Office has an individual emotional component. It is as environmentally sustainable as the traditional houses in the old villages. But nowadays, some solutions and materials have changed in regard to traditional construction. The design and construction solution for the office is strategically designed to be applicable to a wide range of low-cost common-fit projects in urban Vietnam. The entire wall construction is using cement brick, not plastered, instead of the traditional red brick. The floor is polished concrete instead of ceramic tile or granite. The environmental aspect was to reduce the impact of the works to nature, to minimize the total energy used with very low construction works.

TOCA DO URSO – COLORADO
SUPERLIMÃO

Location: Rodovia Anhanguera km 308, Ribeirão Preto, Brazil | **Completion:** 2017 | **Client:** Cervejaria Colorado | **Building type:** commercial | **GFA:** 2,000 m² | **Photos:** Maria Acayaba

Brazilian Colorado Brewery, located in Ribeirão Preto, commissioned the "Toca do Urso" – a space that simulates a bear cave to receive visitors. Designed by Superlimão, this project shows the use of several vernacular and passive techniques to create a pleasant micro-climate ambient in an extremely hot and poorly ventilated region. The architects avoided enclosing the environment and using active air-conditioning techniques. The project sought to take advantage of what already existed in the surroundings, such as the crown of two large trees that shade the area a good part of the day. The large circular hall was buried one and a half meter and the land removed from the ground was relocated creating a three meter slope around the central hall, creating a large barrier of thermal inertia as in the caves. The circular wing-shaped cover with skylight optimizes natural circulation and captures wind in any direction. In the center of the hall is a mirror of water and a set of canals.

Ecological aspects: passive techniques to create pleasant micro-climate ambient | circular wing-shaped roof with skylight optimizes natural circulation and captures wind in any direction | return of ventilation and air-conditioning through grates on the floor | native trees were planted | underground flooded ducts to lower temperature | angle of the roof helps to reflect sound and reduces internal noise | only local materials, within 20 km, were used

All the return of ventilation and air-conditioning happens through grates on the floor that connect these channels so that the air is renewed and humidified, reducing the temperature naturally. The circular format of the Toca do urso is made of gabion walls, which have great absorption and guarantee thermal comfort inside the hall, even when crowded. The environment is open, so the air is renewed through cross ventilation or convection. The water mirror and underground flooded ducts help to humidify, filter the air and reduce the temperature. From a structural point of view Toca do Urso stands out in its shape. By being circular, it allowed the embankment land to be supported by the joint use of prefabricated concrete staves and gabion walls, replacing large structures and valuing techniques of low cost that avoid waste and value labor and local raw materials.

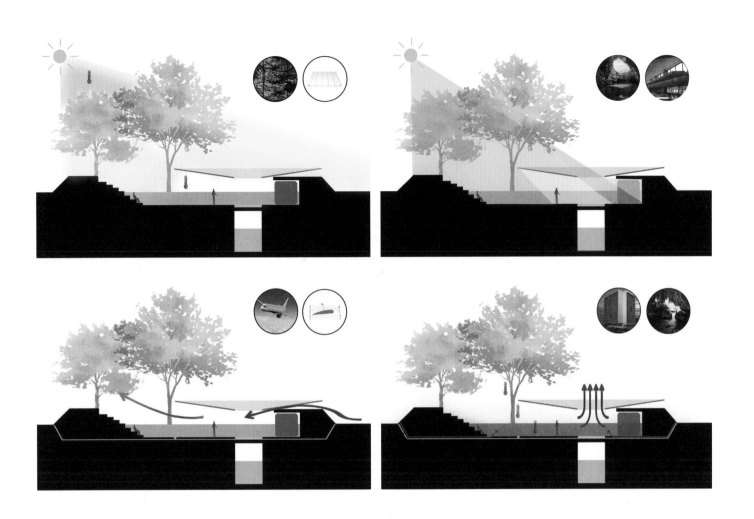

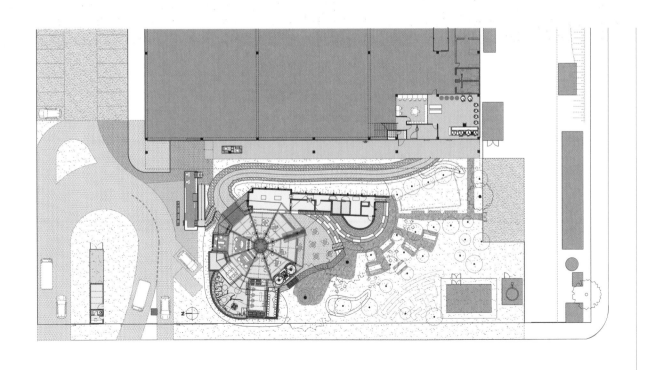

AMHERST COLLEGE
NEW SCIENCE CENTER
PAYETTE

Location: 25 East Drive, Amherst College, Amherst, MA 01002, USA | **Completion:** 2018 | **Client:** Amherst College | **MEP engineering:** Van Zelm, Heywood & Shadford, Inc. | **Landscape architect:** Michael van Valkenburgh Associates | **Building type:** education | **GFA:** 24,000 m² | **Photos:** Robert Benson (130, 133 a. l.), Chuck Choi (133 a. r., b.)

The Science Center is a high-intensity educational laboratory with one of the lowest energy footprints of its building type. Its Site Energy Use Intensity (EUI) has a 76 percent reduction in energy use compared to a typical research building (91 kBtu/year/SF). This rigorously detailed project results from the fusion of design and performance. Aggressive energy use targets and an integrated approach to sustainability began with the earliest planning, impacting everything from programmatic organization to enclosure and mechanical systems designs. The resulting effect is that when operating synergistically, each individual strategy is amplified, increasing the overall beneficial environmental impact. Social and sustainable forces shaped the project's primary gesture, the daylight filled commons. It's unified by the sculptural skylight monitors animating the roofline. They serve multiple roles: cantilevered structural support of the glass curtain wall, acoustic control, balanced north lighting, radiant heating/cooling of the space, and photovoltaic energy production. The photovoltaic array is integrated into the roof monitors above the commons and offsets electric utility consumption of this space. Another ecological aspect concerns the way the building is insulated. A high-performance envelope maintains consistent thermal integrity.

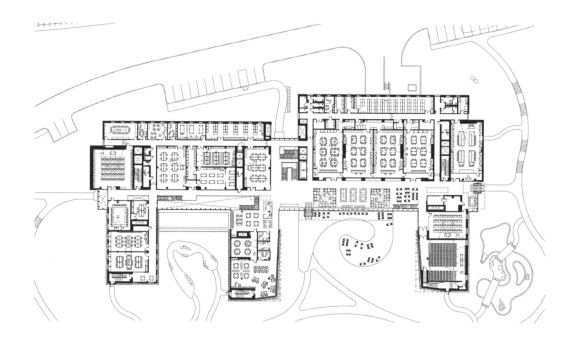

Ecological aspects: PV array monitors offset electric utility consumption | high-performance envelope maintains consistent thermal integrity | double low-e coatings on triple-glazed curtain wall combined with active interior sunshades | multiple energy recovery systems and high-efficiency equipment reduce fossil fuel consumption | non-laboratory sections utilize natural ventilation | rainwater capture diverts potable water consumption from campus cooling systems | concrete structure exposed throughout the building, showcasing inherent materiality and minimizing need for additional finishes | concrete structure allows lower building height and minimizes exterior envelope | infrastructure and HVAC systems promote long-term adaptability and servicing as the needs of researchers and educators evolve over time

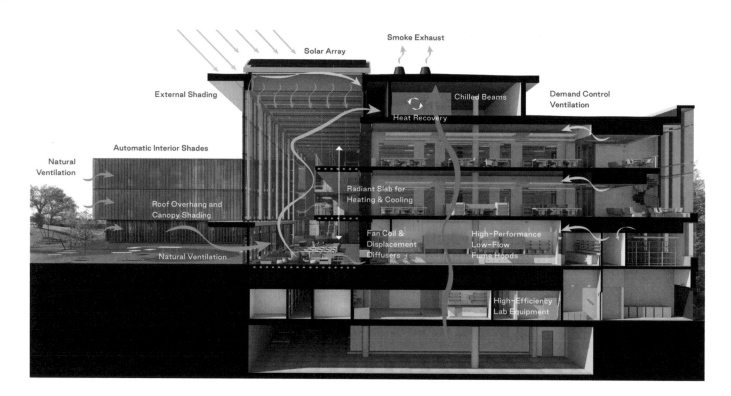

Double low-e coatings on the triple-glazed curtain wall, in combination with active interior sunshades, manage comfort and heat transfers. In addition, several energy recovery systems and highly efficient equipment are combined to reduce the overall consumption of fossil fuels. Natural ventilation is used in the non-laboratory areas of the building. Harvested rainwater is diverted for use in campus cooling systems in lieu of potable drinking water. Passive landscape zones reduce and filter rainwater runoff. Furthermore, the question of the type of material and its simplicity was also emphasized. The concrete structure is exposed throughout the laboratories, corridors and egress stairs, showcasing its inherent materiality and avoiding installation of additional finishes. This structural system also permitted a lower building height, minimizing the exterior envelope.

PARIS COURTHOUSE
RPBW ARCHITECTS

Location: 10, boulevard du Palais, 75001 Paris, France | **Completion:** 2017 | **Client:** Etablissement Public du Palais de Justice de Paris + Bouygues Bâtiment | **Eco engineering:** Eléments Ingénieries | **MEP engineering:** SETEC Bâtiment, Berim | **Landscape design:** C. Guinaudeau, AIA Ingénierie | **Building type:** public | **Site size:** 110,000 m² | **GFA:** 60,000 m² | **Photos:** Joachim Lézie-Cobert (136); Michel Denancé / www.micheldenance.com (137 a. r., b.); Sergio Grazia / www.sergiograzia.fr (134, 135, 137 a. l.)

In June 2017, the French Department of Justice was handed the keys to a major new monument: the Paris Courthouse, designed by Renzo Piano Building Workshop. The glistening 160-meter-high structure is the city's second-tallest building. But, alongside its impressive silhouette, the building also represents a 21st-century vision of justice: one of openness and equality. As always with RPBW's designs, light and clarity were key concerns. For the Courthouse, transparency was especially crucial: For trust and openness to be established, it is essential to see from the outside what is happening inside. All of the building's crystal-clear façades are fully glazed and almost everywhere in the building benefit from direct or indirect natural light, but the focus on luminosity in the 5,000-square-meter public lobby was especially important. Wanting to avoid the dark and intimidating ambiance of a traditional courthouse, the made-to-measure "Justin" lamps hang, like fireflies, from the roof of the pedestal, creating a warm glow. Meanwhile, hand-crafted skylights, flood the atrium with light.

Ecological aspects: heat recovery as primary heat source | 10.5 mW refrigeration production consists of six latest generation magnetic bearing chillers, coupled with adiabatic dry coolers to increase production efficiency | thermofrigo ensures utilization of the permanent heat input for heating | second heating source is CPCU | PV production of 175 mWh/year for covering electricity needs | mechanical ventilation for fresh air with mechanical ventilation stop | natural ventilation automatically controlled by Building Management System thanks to temperature, wind and humidity sensors to ensure optimal use of this cooling | no geothermal energy | rainwater storage in green areas | SYCTOM network: possibility of later connection to the central vacuum collection network

Certificates / standards: French Haute Qualité Environnementale (HQE) certification

The tower of the Courthouse ist broken down into three blocks, with each section divided by a nipped-in "wasp waist" that gives a floating impression. The blocks are tiered, creating a step-like outline that lightens the silhouette of the building, and allows for the creation of the massive roof terraces that soften and green the structure. Environmental concerns were at the forefront of the design initiative. The building's intelligent double-skin façades to the east and west limit energy consumption, while photovoltaic panels contribute to the building's daily energy needs. The green terraces, with nearly 400 trees, help absorb carbon dioxide, while limited parking space encourages the building's estimated 8,800 daily users to use public transport. The building, which respects the goals of the Paris Climate Plan, provides a new benchmark for energy consumption, demonstrating the possibility to create truly green skyscrapers.

WATERHALL PROJECT
ORIENT OCCIDENT ATELIER

Location: Sneung, Battambang, Cambodia | **Completion:** 2019 | **Client:** Sneung Village | **Original architect:** Kenrick Wong, Magic Kwan | **Building type:** infrastructure | **GFA:** 460 m² | **Photos:** Magic Kwan / Kenrick Wong

WaterHall Project, located in Sneung Village of Battambang in Cambodia, is a community hall which houses a pump and filter system that generates clean water for locals. It also mitigates the pollution problem created by plastic bottle waste. The social architecture project won the Hong Kong Institute of Architects (HKIA) Architect Community Project Fund sponsorship. Sneung is a remote village located in the outskirts of Battambang, which was previously ravaged by land mines in the Khmer Rouge era. The village uses a lake nearby and wells as its main water sources.

This means that access to water is very unreliable, as the lake is dry for half of the year, and wells are contaminated by pollution. In order to alleviate the water shortage problem, our team raised funds and created the WaterHall Project. This project sustainably provides safe drinking water to underprivileged communities, whilst creating a social hub to garner social gatherings, celebrations and community festivities.

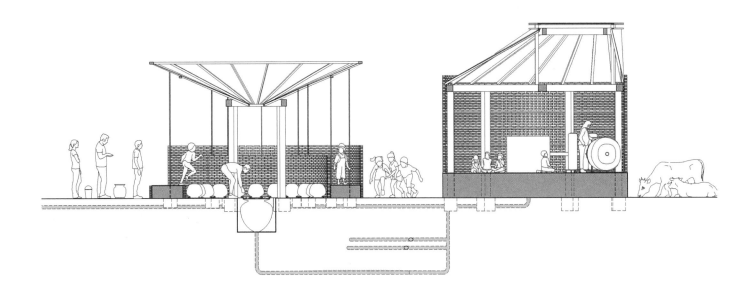

Ecological aspects: filtering rainwater and lake water into potable water | reducing plastic waste | provides community building opportunity | mitigate drought, provides sustainable and ventilated water filtration space

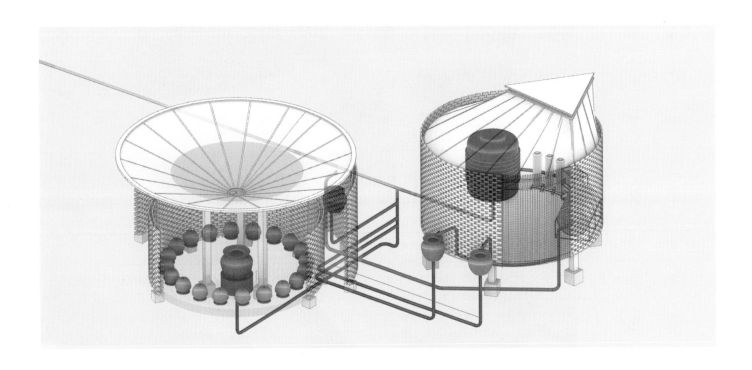

Water is collected from natural rainfall and the nearby lake which is then filtered through a system. With the villagers able to use locally made ceramic jugs and bottles to carry filtered water, the plastic bottle pollution problem is then mitigated. Upon its completion in spring of 2019, the architects were able to get filtered potable water while Battambang was experiencing the worst drought in its recent history. During the design process, local building techniques and methodologies of craft were investigated and documented. Those where employed and expressed with a contemporary language. The hope is that the WaterHall Project can serve as a pilot project, eventually employed around the world. In such a case, local building techniques and methods of craft will change depending on the location, however, an unique contemporary language would always be expressed.

ALNATURA CAMPUS ARBEITSWELT
HAASCOOKZEMMRICH STUDIO2050

Location: Mahatma-Gandhi-Straße 7, 64295 Darmstadt, Germany | **Completion:** 2019 |
Client: Campus 360 GmbH | **Landscape architects:** Ramboll Studio Dreiseitl GmbH | **Clay
building:** Lehm Ton Erde Baukunst GmbH | **Building type:** office | **GFA:** 13,500 m^2 |
Photos: Roland Halbe / www.rolandhalbe.eu

The Working Environment (German: "Arbeitswelt") forms the nucleus of the Alnatura Campus in Darmstadt. On a piece of land, formerly occupied by the Kelley Barracks, a building which follows the principles of holistic and sustainable architecture was created. The Alnatura Working Environment was not designed to impress but instead to invite. It is open towards its environment, for new ideas, and even more importantly, towards people. The atrium is a space that has been designed to breathe, exerting a special pull on everyone inside the building. From the very beginning one design objective had been to achieve natural ventilation of the building throughout

the year and to avoid resource and maintenance intensive heating, ventilation, and air-conditioning systems. The forest towards the west provided ideal conditions for this. The atrium's natural stack effect drives the air circulation – a thermal updraft which is generated beneath the skylight. In unusual weather conditions, such as thermal inversion or thunderstorms, fans inside the air duct can be activated. Thanks to the pre-conditioned air supplied by the earth duct the need for additional heating and cooling is reduced to a minimum.

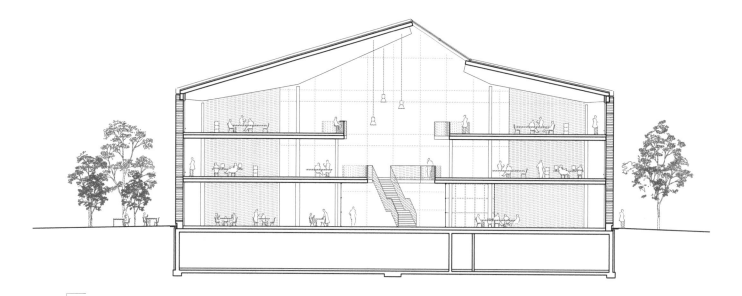

Ecological aspects: materials – wood, loam and untreated concrete – can be reused | energy of the sun harvested by 480 m² roof-mounted PV system | natural ventilation of the building provided by nearby forest | fresh air drawn into subterranean channel by two air intake towers and conveyed into the building | thermal updraft in the atrium | need for additional heating and cooling is reduced to a minimum due to pre-conditioned air supplied by earth duct and integrated loam walls | insulated core: 17 cm of insulation consisting of foam glass gravel | thickness wall: 69 cm, U-value of 0.35 W/(m².K) | loam from Westerwald and recycled from Stuttgart 21 Rail Project | durability loam as material: properties of humidity regulation and thermal storage capacity

Certificates / standards: DGNB Platin standard of the German Deutsche Gesellschaft für Nachhaltiges Bauen

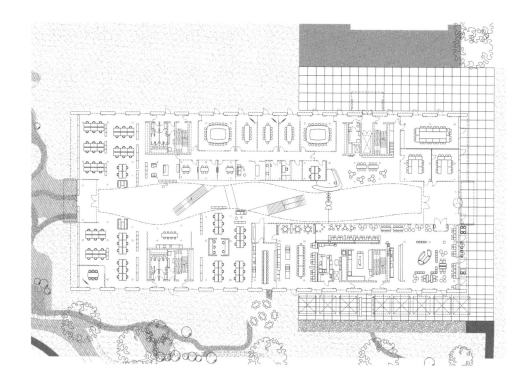

The storage mass of the loam walls and concrete ceiling ensures that the temperature level is stable and balanced. An innovative rammed earth façade was developed together with Martin Rauch and Transsolar. Rammed earth blocks were stacked along the northern and southern façades to form 16 wall segments, each 12 meters high. Here, for the first time in the world, a geothermal wall heating system has been integrated into a dry loam wall. All windows are equipped with glare and sun protection to control the incidence of light also individually. On the sunlit south side of the building, the pond is a natural climate buffer that positively influences the micro-climate of the site in summer. The beautiful tall existing pines on the south side of the building provide the desired shading in the summer. And of course, the sunlight is also used for energy generation via a 480-square-meter photovoltaic system on the roof.

LIVE EDGE RESIDENCE
NATHAN GOOD ARCHITECTS

Location: Deschutes River Ranch, Tumalo, OR 97703, USA | **Completion:** 2018 | **Client:** confidential | **Landscape design:** Heart Springs Landscape Design | **Building type:** residential | **GFA:** 381 m² | **Photos:** Nathan Good (149 a.), Rick Keating

Nestled into a bluff above the scenic Deschutes River in Central Oregon, USA, sits the LEED for Homes, Platinum-certified Live Edge Residence, which combines a modern design aesthetic with an intricate molding to the terrain. The home utilizes extensive exterior terraces for outdoor living and is completed with an attached greenhouse. The home was designed to weave around rock outcroppings and ragged Juniper trees in the arid open-range environment. Sustainable features such as a 23 kWh photovoltaic system, rainwater harvesting, fixed and operable exterior solar shades, PVC-free plumbing, and an electric car charging system integrate modern technology to benefit the environment. The all-electric home has achieved an Energy Performance Score of 0 (zero) as a result of the 21,765 kWh of annual electric generation and an estimated 17,287 kWh of annual electric consumption.

Ecological aspects: 23 kWh solar-electric system with 15 kWh battery back-up system, net-zero energy | insulation: R-68 roof, R-40 walls, R-38 underfloor with six types of insulation | U-0.18 triple-pane windows | heat-recovery ventilation | rainwater harvesting for use in garden | radiant heating | passive heating and cooling | ultra-energy-efficient lighting, appliance and HVAC systems | FSC-certified wood | fire-resistant exterior | wood flooring reclaimed from shipping pallets | non-VOC and formaldehyde-free | durability for environmental resiliency | aging-in-place | designed for low-maintenance | exterior solar shades for natural cooling | on-site food production | passive solar heating with attached greenhouse | exterior insulation to reduce thermal bridging

Certificates / standards: LEED Platinum, 2018 | Earth Advantage Platinum

Sustainable design was not limited to the use of renewable materials and environmentally friendly systems at Live Edge, but also included universal design features. The home's zero-threshold showers, grab bars in every bathroom, 36-inch door openings, wash-let toilets, elevator, ergonomic door and cabinet hardware will contribute to the owner's ability to thrive in place. Live Edge was designed with resilience in mind, enabling the residents to prepare for the unexpected. The 15 kW Tesla Power Wall battery back-up system, an amateur radio tower, wood-burning fireplace, 1,800-gallon potable water cistern, and attached greenhouse provide a multitude of self-sustaining resources for the occupants.

STARR ATRIUM
LPA DESIGN STUDIOS

Location: 1 Edwards Way, Irvine, CA 92614, USA | **Completion:** 2017 | **Client:** Edwards Lifesciences |
Building type: corporate | **GFA:** 2,349 m² | **Photos:** Cris Costea / www.costeaphoto.com

The key element of the campus renovation for Edwards Lifesciences, an industry-leading medical device manufacturer, is the LEED Platinum, 25,000-square-foot Starr Atrium. The Starr Atrium creates a bridge between two existing office buildings, as well as a dramatic new entry to the corporate headquarters. LPA's architects and engineers designed a unique truss-net structural system that spans the space and maximizes its openness. The customized structure also casts an artistic weave shadow across the interior, filtering the light streaming through the skylight that runs the length of the atrium. Floor-to-ceiling windows provide a connection to the outdoors, while a bi-fold vertical lift door can be opened to promote natural ventilation and the use of natural daylight for illumination.

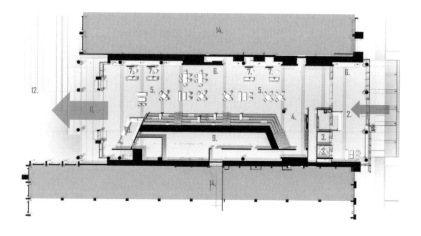

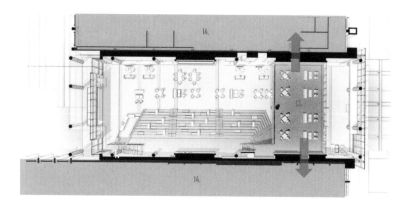

1. Atrium entry
2. Reception / check-in
3. Meeting rooms
4. Museum display
5. Open collaboration / Event space
6. Media screen
7. Digital collaborative spaces
8. Stadium collaborative and event seating
9. Storage area (below stadium)
10. Coffee bar / Service area
11. Vertical bi-fold door (connection to open space)
12. Campus open space
13. Bridge mezzanine collaborative space
14. Existing two-level office/ R&D building

Ecological aspects: solar electricity offsets 100 % of building's energy use | displacement ventilation | natural daylight | sustainably-sourced materials | flexible design supports multiple uses and configurations

Certificates / standards: LEED NC Platinum

The atrium operates at net zero, with a photovoltaic array that fully offsets the energy used by the space. The atrium also includes a variety of conservation measures, such as a displacement ventilation system and LED lighting with controls designed to minimize the project's energy use. As an infill structure between two existing buildings, the reduced envelope was optimized with rigid insulation, a "cool roof" membrane and one inch insulated high-performance glazing. Sustain-

ably-sourced materials were used throughout the project, and the surrounding landscaped area incorporates bioretention planter areas to clean and conserve stormwater runoff. The flexible design of the Starr Atrium supports multiple uses and configurations, while providing an open, collaborative gathering space for the company's 4,000 employees.

JENSON-DELEEUW
NET-ZERO ENERGY HOUSE
PAUL LUKEZ ARCHITECTURE

Location: Harvard, MA, USA | **Completion:** 2018 | **Client:** Richard Jenson and Pat DeLeeuw | **Eco engineering:** Norian / Siani Engineering Inc., Solworks, Deap Energy Group | **Landscape architect:** SegoDesign | **Building type:** residential | **GFA:** 240 m² | **Photos:** Greg Premru / www.gregpremru.com

This 2,000-square-foot home is designed for a recently retired couple, a math professor and a provost. It's located on a bucolic two-acre site in Harvard, Massachusetts. The couple's energy needs for the house and their electric car are provided entirely by the sun. The home's design uses passive design principles, Photovoltaic panels, a battery storage system, and an electric car. The lease on the vehicle is paid for by extra energy produced and sent to the grid, essentially paying for the vehicle in full. The special location of the house is deliberately chosen. Carefully locating the house on the site's highest elevations captures as much sun as possible. The profile of the roof and its solar array also optimizes solar gain. The 56 photovoltaic panel system generates 21,000 kWh a year. Surplus energy is stored in the two 16 kWh batteries, providing uninterrupted energy on cloudy days or evenings. The Sonnen battery system directs power to the house and car as needed throughout the day. Excess energy not stored in the battery is sent to the grid. The heating and cooling system uses three mini–split systems.

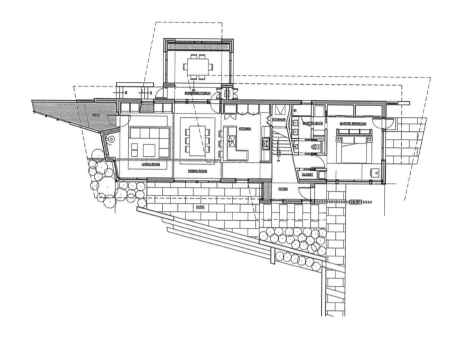

Ecological aspects: PV panels | two 16 kWh battery storage systems | empowering an electric car | insulated walls measuring 1 ft thick and low-infiltration detailing optimize heat retention | heating and cooling by a ducted mini-split system | deep roof overhang to avoid overheating | triple-glazed windows | fuel-fired unit heater | balanced ventilation system: HRV, 88 cfm, 26.0 watts | most materials are sustainable, recyclable, durable, and carbon-storing, like porcelain floor, metal roof, wood and steel finishes | materials act as thermal mass | infiltration rate heating: 960, cooling: 960 CFM50 (method used: blower door test) | most products designed for at least 15–25+ years | internal rate of return for renewable energy and battery system exceeds 10 % over 12 years, with a payback period of 9.36 years | sited to optimize generation of energy from the sun

Certificates / standards: American HERS rating (-23)

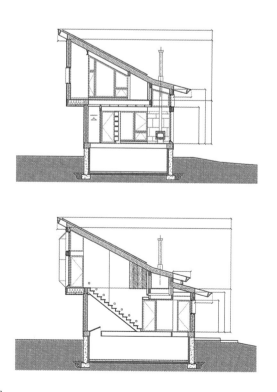

The south-facing wall's expansive windows flood the interiors with light and wintertime heat. Deep roof overhangs shield the interior from overheating in the summer. High ceilings enable ventilation throughout the house. In winter, triple-glazed windows, 12-inch insulated walls, and low-infiltration detailing contain the house's heat. A wood stove supplements the heat on sub-zero days. By using market-ready renewable energy systems and passive design strategies, this design demonstrates that homes can be designed to achieve net-zero energy or better, even powering a homeowner's electric vehicles. Conceived holistically, the performance and comfort of such homes provide homeowners considerable advantages over traditional market designed housing.

THE CURVE
ARCHITEKTEN | K2

Location: Neuenhofstraße 180, 52078 Aachen, Germany | **Completion:** 2019 | **Client:** Dr. Babor GmbH & Co. KG | **Building type:** corporate | **GFA:** 7,200 m² | **Photos:** Olaf Rohl / www.olaf-rohl.de

The Curve was planned with sustainability in mind and thus corresponds to Dr. Babor's corporate philosophy with regard to sustainable and resource-saving products. In order to optimize the energy balance of the building, a dynamic building simulation was carried out during the planning phase. The results of this simulation lead to a performance-oriented and efficient design of the heating and cooling systems, thus reducing energy requirements and costs while also taking into account the optimal and comfortable indoor climate conditions desired by the users. The build-ing's heating and cooling requirements are mainly covered by geothermal energy. For this purpose, 36 boreholes up to 100 meters below the building access geothermal energy. Here, heat is extracted from the ground to supply the building's heating/ cooling ceilings in winter; in summer, the ground is used passively as a cold energy source. Further-more, a gas-fired combined heat and power unit is used in the building, which covers peak heat loads in winter and generates electricity in the process.

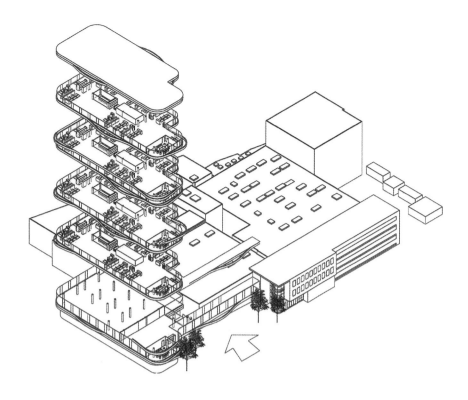

Ecological aspects: use of renewable energies of the surroundings | thermal insulation glazing | sun protection lamella venetian blinds | geothermal energy | green roofs | PV | cooling ceilings | planting with greenery and flowering plants | water basins for micro-climate | recyclable aluminum extrusions | pollutant-free materials: carpeting, paint, etc. | highly flexible floor plan design

Certificates / standards: German KfW 55 standard

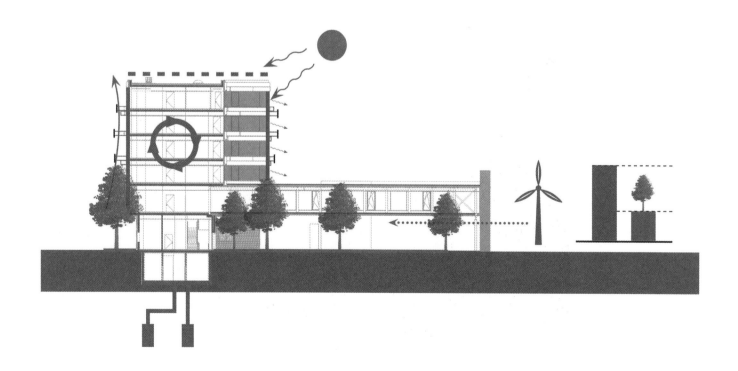

To optimize operating times, a connection was created to the existing administrative and production buildings on site, which require thermal energy all year round. The primary energy demand according to EnEV of the building is given as 496 mWh/a. Thus, the building has been constructed as an KfW 55 building and requires less than 55 percent of the legally permissible primary energy demand. The façade was designed with circumferential and horizontally swinging façade bands, whose attachment is partly based on up to 20 meters long and 2.5 meters cantilevered bands. In order to connect the already existing administration to the new building, a transparent skywalk was designed, which connects the two parts of the building with a span of 40 meters – without any support.

SHELL HOUSE / THE LANGUAGE
OF THE FOREST
TONO MIRAI ARCHITECTS

Location: Nagano, Japan | **Completion:** 2018 | **Eco engineering:** Masuda structural design office |
Building type: residential | **GFA:** 58.04 m² | **Photos:** Takeshi Noguchi

Shell House is a small villa in the forest of Nagano which is located in center of Japan. The client demanded for an architecture that is unusual, beautiful, and does not make you feel old in time. Strict conditions were also the retreat line by the landscape regulation and the building volume ratio of 20 percent of the 290-square-meter site. Behind the house runs a small road from where you have a view of the back of the house. On the other side, the house opens onto a small watercourse. The house fits into its surroundings both in form and materiality. It merges with the surrounding nature. In order to build as environmentally friendly as possible, regional wood species were used that meet the international PEFC standard: the Program for the Endorsement of Forest Certification Schemes. In addition, work was done with earth and, as far as possible, by hand. Petrochemical materials were deliberately avoided. All the interior rooms are finished with local earth and wood.

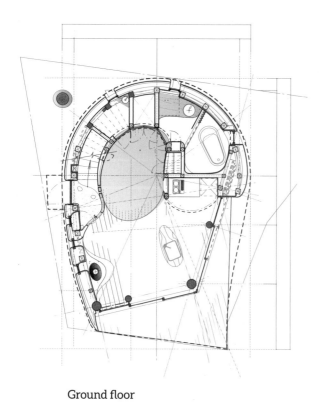

Ground floor

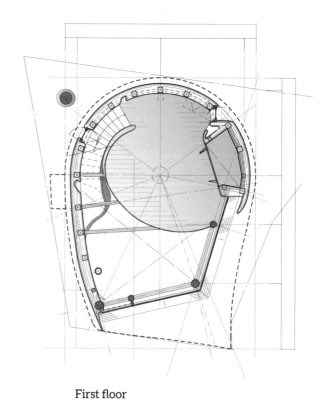

First floor

Ecological aspects: insulation with sheep wool, cedar bark board | U-value of wall 0.207, of ceiling 0.126 | vertical natural ventilation: ground floor big window with wood sliding door to first floor, opened skylight and dome form | passive design: summer sunlight cut by long eaves, winter sunlight goes directly to earth wall and heat it through transom glass windows | interior earth wall heat storage, moisture control and breathing | recycable natural materials: interior earth wall not using lime, solid woods are able to be recycled and renaturated untoxic | rammed earth fireplace | firewood as recycable energy | chestnut wood deck on the ground floor for durability | low embodied energy: local clay and woods from within 100 km | all structural woods are Japanese forest certification SGEC, equal with international standard PEFC | load reduction for human and environment: used woods are all solid | construction management: architect has moved to live near the construction field and check the process in detail | local landscape conditions for retreat: building area and floor area <20 %, setback: 3 m from boundary, 5 m from road; eaves length >500 mm, roof cline >2.0 / 10

Certificates / standards: Japanese CASBEE 5 stars

The earth wall of the curved surface gently stretches across the whole. When drawing in the south-east wooden fittings, it becomes integrated with the forest through the wood deck. On the ground floor, there is a kitchen, as well as a bathroom. A winding staircase leads to the first floor, which is open plan. This house is designed according to passive design. Outside wall, roof and ceiling average heat transmission coefficient. The Japanese environmental assessment and satisfying the primary energy consumption standards in Japan includes a reduction of 11 percent. The earth wall is combined with 180-millimeter wool insulation. Seven beams born from the organic earth wall have expressed the cycle of life of the human and universe and the two inscribed circles represent the correspondence of them. It is the architecture talked to human born from and return to earth.

CIASA AQUA BAD CORTINA
PEDEVILLA ARCHITECTS

Location: Strada Fanes 40, 39030 St. Vigil in Enneberg, Italy | **Completion:** 2020 | **Client:** family Alberti-Mutschlechner, Aqua Bad Cortina Hotel & Thermal Baths | **Eco engineering:** Ing. Paolo Orrù, Schlanders | **Building type:** residential | **GFA:** 160 m² | **Photos:** Gustav Willeit / www.guworld.com

The ciAsa – the word ciasa means house in Rhaeto-Romanic language – is a high alpine solid wood residential house in the South Tyrolean village of St. Vigil, surrounded by the Gadertal Dolomites. The building is based on the archaic form of a house, where no distinction is made between roof and façade. The rising form of the roof makes the building visible from afar, while at the same time the roof takes on a protective position due to its low eaves line. The shape of the trapezoid appears as a recurring element in the overall design. The trapezoidal dormer windows as well as a skylight, whose light falls conically into the house, serve to illuminate the interior. The three above-ground floors are entirely made of wood from the sur-rounding forests: The load-bearing structure is made of spruce wood, the interior surfaces and the custom-made furniture are made of solid hand-planed Swiss stone pine. Due to its warm shade and characteristic smell, which gives the room a feeling of well-being and warmth, Swiss stone pine has been used in local tradition for centuries for the interior lining of the living room. The façade is clad like a cone with hand-split larch shingles. Great importance is attached to the aspect of sustainability and regionality: local materials, processed by local craftsmen. In addition, synthetic materials were avoided.

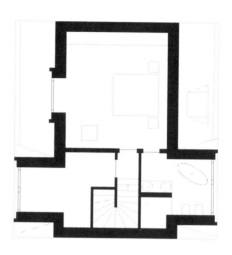

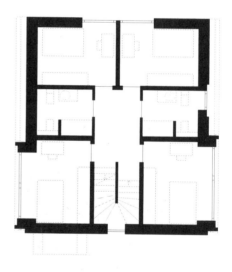

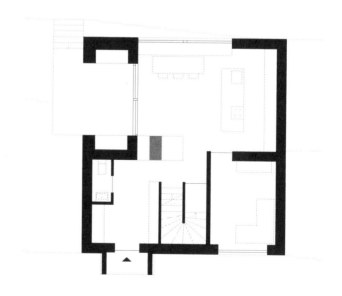

Ecological aspects: building shell made of solid wood, no insulation | daylight entry by controlled window setting that reacts to the course of the day and the climate | controlled living space ventilation | moon wood of the storm Vaja from October 30th, 2018 processed on site | erratic blocks of dolomite rock | hand-planed surfaces | no surfaces to be maintained | façade made of hand-split larch shingles permanently weatherproof without any further surface treatment | flexible because of its symmetrical floor plan | shortest transport routes: concrete mix on site from stream material with in-house thermal water | local craftsmen

Certificates / standards: Italian Klimahaus A

The concrete for the basement consists of dolomite rock from the passing stream, enriched with the house's own thermal water. Due to the overall generous wall thickness, a very low heat transfer value was achieved, which is why additional insulation was completely unnecessary. Not only the wood of the house is local, but also the stone for the floors and bathrooms, which was cut from dolomite boulders, comes from the surrounding mountains. The choice of materials was determined both by aesthetic qualities and the knowledge of their resistance and durability. Great importance was also payed to the social and cultural aspects of sustainability. Only craftsmen from Gadertal were hired, who were able to enrich the project with their experience and expertise in local construction methods.

TAIKOO HUI (GZ) SUSTAINABLE WASHROOM
IDA&BILLY ARCHITECTS

Location: 383 Tianhe Road, Tian He Zhong Xin, Tianhe District, Guangzhou, China | **Completion:** 2015 | **Client:** Taikoo Hui (Guangzhou) Development | **Building type:** commercial | **GFA:** 580 m² | **Photos:** Ida&Billy Architects

The sustainable design toilet series aims to raise the environmental awareness in the public realm and to become the role model of sustainability in the commercial and retail sector. A bright grotto – a contemporary abstraction of nature – to refresh shoppers amidst delicate garments and dazzling commodities is the design concept for this underground toilet. The design aims to tie back to nature, formally as well as environmentally. Sustainability, spatial sculpting and human comfort drive the whole design. Minimum alterations are made to the original layout to minimize structural and

piping alteration. The round and tilted square columns are exposed and painted to form a homogeneous white mass to engage the space with unique shape and angle that hint the underlining structures. White 'cyclorama' setting is applied to give a bright, clean ambient, and eliminate dark, dirty edges. Walls join the ceiling seamlessly with recyclable glass fiber reinforced gypsum curved panel, to diffuse light for plants and as general lighting.

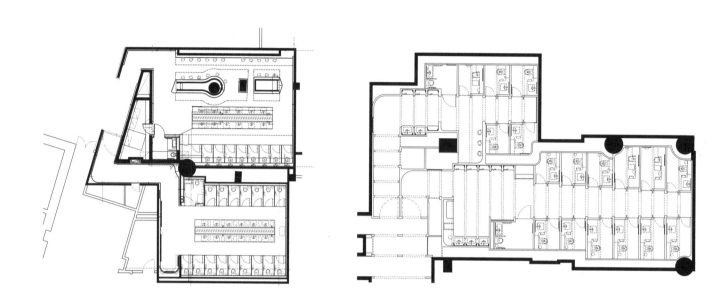

Ecological aspects: waterless urinal | water-saving toilet and vacuum toilet save up to 80 % water, reduce waste up to 90 % | LED lighting fixture in washroom and baby caring room saves electrical consumption and maintenance cost | two fans to enhance fresh air movement, replace mechanical cooling in winter and reduce cooling load in summer | indoor plants to purify air, raise indoor oxygen level | glass-reinforced gypsum as post-consumer recycled material | minimum alterations to original efficient layout, to minimize structural and piping alteration | floor: newly-casted dark-gray terrazzo stone | original sandstone and gray tiles crushed as aggregates for new terrazzo, forming unique golden chips revealing the idea of recycling | panels made to size and designed to minimize excessive framing | irrigation utilizes gray water collected from the wash basins, supported by local filtration system | water tap with integrated hand dryer for sustainability and cleanness, avoiding dripping water on counter-top and floor, saves space and paper towels

Certificates / standards: LEED EBOM Platinum for TaiKoo Hui Mall

The premium Sustainable Washroom aims to create an experience of outdoor alleys and plaza – a reminiscence to European elegance and fineness. Layering and arches are used to give an unifying and intricate framework. The arches contract and expand to give spaces of different dimensions. The journey starts with two defined arch doorways, each leads into an alley of arches. The alley turns, and the arches expand into a plaza – the common dressing. Wash basins and make-up counters are expressed as insertions between the layers, black metal frames to highlight and to give a prestigious definition. The journey continues into a lane with street lights and doorways on both sides and plants hanging from above. The arch continues to inside the private realms of the individual cubicles and gives an intimate atmosphere. The forest of arches accompanies the whole journey, giving a variety of silhouettes yet a unifying experience.

BLOOMBERG
FOSTER + PARTNERS

Location: 3 Queen Victoria Street, London EC4N 4TQ, Great Britain | **Completion:** 2017 | **Client:** Bloomberg LP | **Building type:** office | **GFA:** 102,190 m² | **Photos:** James Newton / www.jnphotographs.co.uk (177 a., b.), Nigel Young / Foster + Partners

Bloomberg's new European headquarters is the world's most sustainable office building. The development scored 99.1 percent against the latest BREEAM sustainability rating scheme, achieving an Outstanding rating. This is the highest design-stage score ever achieved by any major office development in the world. Innovation in sustainability is at the heart of the Bloomberg building's design, from its engineering to its construction and intended use. Compared to a typical office building, its environmental strategies deliver a 73 percent saving in water consumption and a 35 percent saving in energy consumption and associated CO_2 emissions. At 600 tons per annum, this CO_2 reduction equates to driving a domestic car 120 times around the globe. The main contributors to energy saving are the building's innovative power, lighting, water and ventilation systems. Unlike standard office lighting, the bespoke ceiling panels at Bloomberg's new London building combine heating, cooling, lighting and acoustic functions. An on-site Combined Heat and Power (CHP) generation center supplies heat and power in a single, efficient system with reduced carbon emissions. Natural gas is converted to power and the waste heat generated in the process is also used in the building either for heating and hot water, or to generate cooling, via an absorption chiller for Bloomberg's technical facilities.

Heat   Power

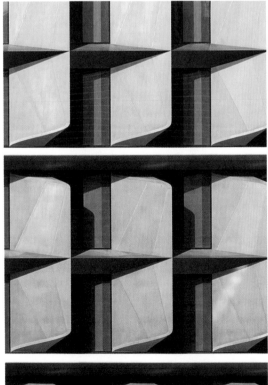

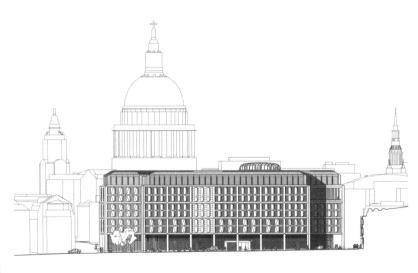

Ecological aspects: 73 % saving in water consumption; rainwater recycling and net-zero mains water for flushing; 25 million liters of water saved each year | 117 blades open and close for natural ventilation; reduced dependency on mechanical ventilation and cooling equipment | smart airflow: smart CO_2 sensing controls dynamically adjust airflow based on occupancy; expected to save 600–750 mWh of power per annum; projected to reduce carbon emissions by 300 metric tons per year | 35 % overall saving in energy consumption | on-site Combined Heat and Power generation center | lightning with 40 % less energy than a typical fluorescent office light system

Certificates / standards: BREEAM – Outstanding certified

Taking advantage of the City's dense environment, the building's façades are naturally shaded by neighboring buildings. In addition, large bronze blades provide solar shading to inner spaces. When ambient weather conditions are temperate, these blades can open and close, allowing the building to operate in a "breathable" natural ventilation mode. Natural air flows through the building, up its atrium and out of the roof with the central ramp acting as a chimney. Reducing dependency on mechanical ventilation and cooling equipment significantly reduces energy consumption. The ability to dynamically adjust airflow in response to occupancy hours and patterns results in significant energy reduction benefits. Smart CO_2 sensing controls allow air to be distributed according to the approximate number of people occupying each zone of the building at any given time. Rainwater from the roof, cooling tower blow-off water, and gray water sources, like basins and showers, are captured, treated and recycled. Collectively, thanks to these water conservation strategies, the Bloomberg building uses roughly 70 percent less potable.

TAOYUAN AGRICULTURE EXPO GREENHOUSE 1 & 2
BIAS ARCHITECTS & ASSOCIATES

Location: Xinwu District, Taoyuan City, Taiwan | **Completion:** 2018/2019 | **Client:** Taoyuan City | **Original architect:** Hanju Chen, Tammy Liu, Alessandro Martinelli | **Building type:** temporary | **GFA:** 336 m² | **Photos:** Rex Chu (180 b. r.), Rockburger

The project is a temporary installation that follows a public competition for a pavilion dedicated to the concept of greenhouse and new ways of sustainability. This was held in the context of the Taoyuan Agriculture Expo 2018. Due to particular circumstances, the pavilion has been preserved for one year, and it has been the subject of conversion and a second installment during the following Taoyuan Agriculture Expo 2019, where the 'return to nature' of the building was showcased. In particular, since BIAS Architects engages both architecture design and curating, the pavilion's

first installment was organized according to the possibility of creating different climatic zones by specific technologies and passive architectural solutions. Within these zones, it was possible to host both different planting and different human activities, therefore to showcase their possible interactions and mutualism.

The second installment showcased the possibility of dismantling the structure and exploiting specific plants, such as the herbs, to control the return of an architectural site to nature. Indeed, both installments aimed to demonstrate new relations between man, nature, and architecture, which include both aspects of their life and project. The various architectural elements were assembled to be dismantled and recycled later. Clips, clamps, and movable joints were used instead of wielding. The pavilion was designed to be possibly converted, and this was later done.

Ecological aspects: insulation: various greenhouse membranes, including anti-UV films and metal meshes, differently combined in order to achieve different degrees of solar protection | various technologies, including air exchangers and humidifiers, and passive architecture solutions combined to achieve different climatic zones

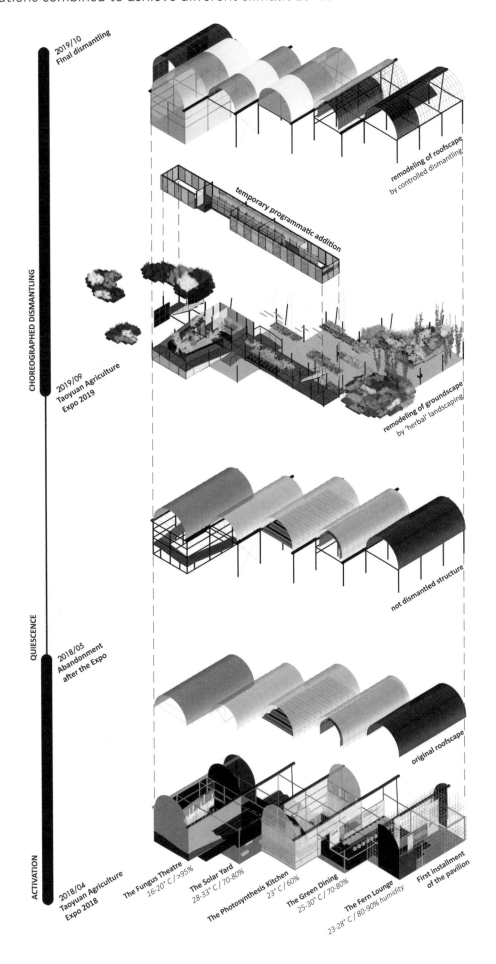

2019/10
Final dismantling

CHOREOGRAPHED DISMANTLING

remodeling of roofscape
by controlled dismantling

temporary programmatic addition

2019/09
Taoyuan Agriculture
Expo 2019

remodelling of groundscape
by 'herbal' landscaping

QUIESCENCE

not dismantled structure

2018/05
Abandonment
after the Expo

original roofscape

ACTIVATION

2018/04
Taoyuan Agriculture
Expo 2018

The Fungus Theatre
16-20° C / >95%

The Solar Yard
28-33° C / 70-80%

The Photosynthesis Kitchen
23° C / 60%

The Green Dining
25-30° C / 70-80%

The Fern Lounge
23-28° C / 80-90% humidity

First installment
of the pavilion

[181]

ARCTIC SAUNA PAVILION
TONI YLI-SUVANTO ARCHITECTS

Location: Lapland, Finland | **Completion:** 2019 | **Client:** confidential | **Building type:** leisure | **GFA:** 50 m² | **Photos:** Toni Yli-Suvanto Architects / www.toniylisuvanto.com

In Lapland, the extent of living indoor space used to follow a cycle of natural seasons. During cold wintertime, the occupied indoor space was limited to one compact building with an efficient multi-use floor plan, in order to save heating resources. In warmer seasons the living area was expanded into several unheated buildings with different specific purposes, arranged around the common courtyard. This way the lifestyle in summer was spacious and the main building was prevented from getting overheated. This pavilion follows this tradition by creating a hub for social activities during the warmer seasons and a buffer for expanded living space when required. In terms of massing and horizontal orientation, the building is a fusion of two geometrical orders: It follows the regular orthogonal geometry of the existing built context in the northern hill side, but in the southern lake side it takes reference of the organic geometry of the natural shoreline. In terms of vertical geometry, the walls are tilted outwards following the traditional way of constructing storage buildings in Lapland – just like the two existing storage buildings near the pavilion – preventing the timber wall construction from getting wet. Cooking and dining take place in the unheated main space, dominated by generous views towards the Nordic lake landscape in the south-west, and towards the midnight sun in the north.

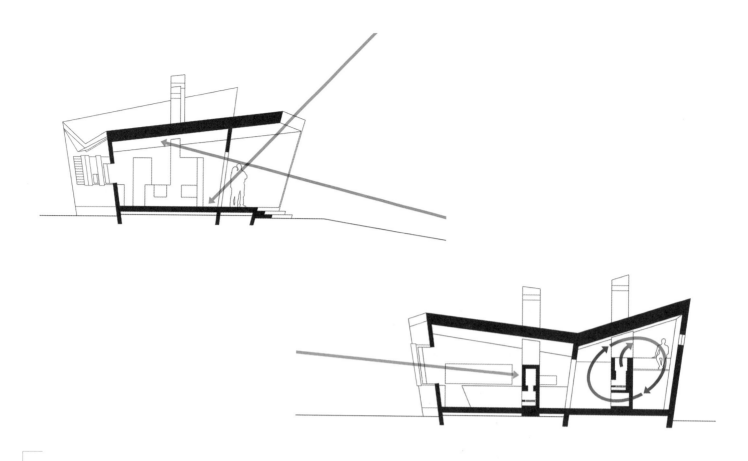

Ecological aspects: heating by local wood | recycled cellulose-based insulation | natural heat and humidity circulation in the sauna space | passive indoor temperature control | local reuse of nutrients of biological waste in the garden | solid log from local sustainably-harvested forest | locally-sourced and recycled gravel | timber fiber based sealant | multi-use social space for cooking, dining, cooling down, entertainment, relaxing | 95 % of all material sourced and processed locally | passive biological gray water treatment

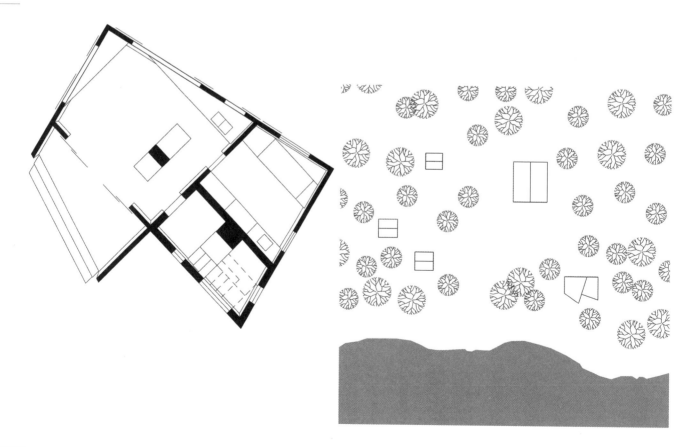

The lake view is captured by the main opening, operated and adjusted by sliding doors, and framed by a covered terrace extension. Reflected sunlight from the lake surface is directed to the space by a generous tilted ceiling surface. Social activities are complemented by the sauna room, where bathing and relaxation takes place within the same space, following an ancient arctic concept. This way the hot air in the sauna is more humid and optimized for the sauna experience, and excess construction for separate rooms are avoided, saving scarce resources. The sauna geometry follows the principle of natural air flow and enhances the optimal movement of hot steams: Bathing takes place on cooler lower level, while hot steams and views to the lake are enjoyed higher in the same room.

EL MAQUI HOUSE
GITC ARCHITECTURE

Location: El Maqui road, Olmué, Chile | **Completion:** 2014 | **Client:** Jessica González | **Further participants:** Carlos Estay and Rodrigo del Castillo | **Eco engineering:** Anthony Behm | **Landscape design:** GITC & Sakura | **Original architect:** Rodrigo Belmar Expósito, Felipe Vera Buschmann | **Building type:** residential | **GFA:** 253 m² | **Photos:** Felipe Díaz Contardo

The building is located in the eastern hillside of El Maqui Brook, a rural place of the Coastal Mountain Range of Chile. This geographical zone is part of a protected natural reserve with high ecological value because of its singular and diverse coexisting ecosystems. The client asked for a seasonal house for a family of six and a garden around the house whose principal element was water. In order not to alter the rich forests and ecosystems GITC sought an already damaged hillside without vegetation to construct the building. The new landscaping project should recover the area. The eastern hillside position assures prolonged sunlight and optimal exposure to the prevailing ascendant air current.

The program distribution, the volume and the way it stands over the ground response to two opposite situations: A preexisting one – the geography and weather – and a proposed one – the near garden and the water. A dormitory pavilion rises with presence and exposure, oriented to the views. The common areas volume adopts an intimate and hermetic position focused on the family activities and on its direct relationship with the garden and water. The water surfaces that round the house were dimensioned by a swimming pool request and by a proposed bio-filter pond with carefully thought-out levels and extensions.

Ecological aspects: solar electricity | mineral wool and ventilated façade | passive temperature control | bio-filter pond | biological sewage treatment | natural ventilation optimization | passive drying system on native timber | solar and predominant wind criteria for distribution of volumes | gray water reuse with earthworms treatment system

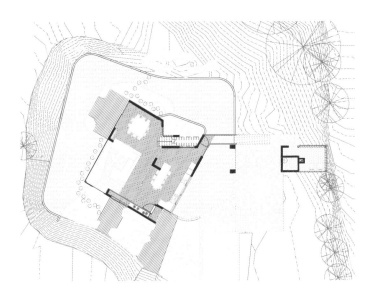

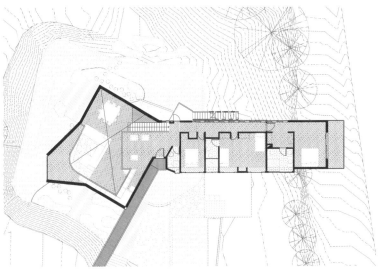

The water surfaces and its specific aquatic plants made a flooded garden possible, excavated on the hillside, directly in contact with the internal common area. The garden also provides an important fresh air supply necessary to control and manage the high summer temperatures. The reinforced concrete of the retaining and bearing walls was built on site by a overlap table formwork system. The reinforced concrete has a tectonic and solid expression on the one hand. On the other hand its textures, imperfections and shadows make it human, provide a friendly relationship with the habitants. The second level responds to an efficient construction system. The steel frame structure allowed to satisfy formal requirements and get light and simple ventilated wooden solutions for the building enclosures to control the heat.

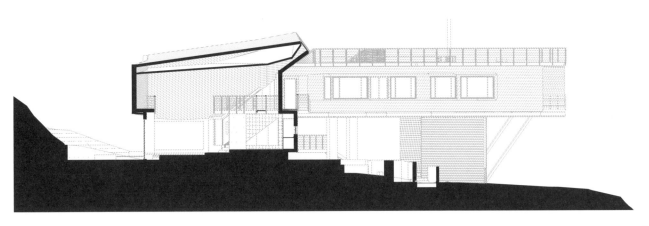

INDEX